DISCIPLINE WITHOUT SHOUTING OR SPANKING

JERRY WYCKOFF, PH.D
BARBARA C. UNELL

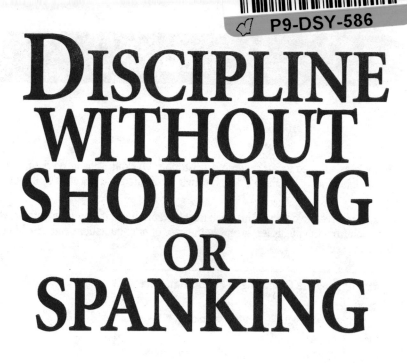 Meadowbrook Press

Distributed by Simon & Schuster
New York

Distributed in the UK by
Chris Lloyd Sales and Marketing

DEDICATION

This book is dedicated to our children, Christopher Wyckoff, Allison Wyckoff, Justin Alex Unell, and Amy Elizabeth Unell, for their unsolicited and priceless contributions to this book.

Library of Congress Cataloging in Publication Data

Wyckoff, Jerry, 1935-
 Discipline without shouting or spanking.

 Includes index.
 1. Discipline of children—Handbooks, manuals,
 etc.
I. Unell, Barbara, 1951- . II. Title.
HQ770.4.W93 1984 649'.64 84-527

 ISBN 0-88166-019-1 (priced)
 S & S Ordering Number 0-671-54464-0

©1984 by Jerry Wyckoff and Barbara C. Unell

Published by Meadowbrook Press, 18318 Minnetonka Boulevard, Deephaven, MN 55391.

BOOK TRADE DISTRIBUTION by Simon & Schuster, a division of Simon and Schuster, Inc., 1230 Avenue of the Americas, New York, NY 10020.

S & S Ordering Number: 0-671-54464-0

First published in the UK 1991.

DISTRIBUTION IN THE UK AND IRELAND by Chris Lloyd Sales and Marketing, P.O. Box 327, Poole, Dorset BH15 2RG.

Text Design: Tabor Harlow
Cover Design: Erik Broberg

97 96 95 94   23 22 21 20

Printed in the United States of America

TABLE OF CONTENTS

ACKNOWLEDGMENTS

We would like to thank Tom Grady for his support and encouragement throughout the creation of *Discipline Without Shouting or Spanking*. We'd also like to thank the following people without whom this book would still be a twinkling in our eyes: Ray Peekner; Robert Unell; Millie Wyckoff; Candace Hanlon; William Cameron, M.D.; Margaret Baldwin; the Greater Kansas City Mothers of Twins Club; Linda Surbrook; Laura Bloent; Michelle Lange; Edie Nelson; Josephine B. Coleman; Valerie Bielsker; Kathy Mohn; Wilma Yeo; and all the parents who have brought their problems to our attention and taken the time and had the tenacity to solve them with us.

PREFACE

All children—and especially preschoolers—create discipline problems, no matter how perfect the children or parents might be. Both well-adjusted and not-so-well-adjusted children of every race, color, creed, economic background, and social status have needs and wants, just as their parents have wants and expectations for them. When these needs and wants don't fit together like puzzle pieces and preschoolers don't see eye-to-eye with their parents, problems arise.

But the overwhelming problems of parenting can often at least be minimized when parents learn how to match their parenting skills with their preschoolers' needs. This book offers practical remedies for the common behavior problems of normal, healthy one- to five-year-olds—remedies that parents and caregivers can apply in the heat of the conflicts that arise during the normal course of family life. Our intent is to show parents how to react to discipline problems in calm, consistent, and effective ways—without shouting or spanking. We want to turn parents into "disciplined parents" who can control themselves when their children are least in control.

The approach we take in this book combines the best of two worlds, professional and parental. It is written by parents of toddlers, preteenagers, and adolescents, who back up the business of problem-solving with facts— professional, researched data presented without theoretical jargon. Over the past twenty years, we have collectively studied developmental and child psychology at the university level; served on the psychological staff of a state hospital for children and as a psychologist in a major suburban school district; conducted numerous parent groups and national seminars and workshops; been consultants to school districts and mental health centers; taught psychology at the university level; written extensively about parents and children; and raised a total of four children.

The problem-solving principles and the disciplining strategies that we propose here are based on data derived from the behavioral psychology movement of the 1960s and '70s, which studied the behavior of children in "real" settings that were common to most children—homes, schools, and playgrounds. Behavioral psychology is oriented toward offering practical solutions to common problems and to measuring the effectiveness of these solutions.

We designed this book to be a handy reference for parents who are faced with the daily problems of parenting—sort of a first-aid book for handling misbehavior. It recognizes the need parents have for brevity, for immediacy, and for direct, practical answers to parenting questions. The book offers advice on how to prevent misbehavior problems from occuring and how to solve them when they do. It also presents "case histories" that illustrate how a number of fictionalized families have used the strategies outlined in the book to handle real problems.

Note: Please read the developmental milestones (pages 9 to 10) before applying the do's and don'ts. Doing so will help you understand the general behavior characteristics of one- to five-year-olds before mistakenly deciding that these characteristics are abnormal or before erroneously blaming yourself for causing your child's misbehavior. For example, in order to understand the motivations behind your two-year-old's always saying no, it is helpful to know that negativism is part of a normally developing two-year-old's behavior. This information will help you determine whether a certain kind of behavior is a problem in your family circle.

WHO IS A PRESCHOOLER?

Those awesome, metamorphic days and nights during which a one-year-old child seems to suddenly become a five-year-old miniature adult are called the preschool years within this book. A *preschooler* here refers to a child not yet into a formal school experience, and includes toddlers, but not infants.

Newborn infants and babies under one are unique creatures who are primarily governed by needs (for food and sleep and human contact) that are generally met by basic physical and emotional nurturance, not through strategies that are psychological in nature. For this reason, this book primarily focuses on the post-infancy child, whose developmental needs lend themselves to parental training.

INTRODUCTION

The preschool years are the prime physical, emotional, and intellectual learning years of life. At their best, preschoolers are curious, inventive, eager, and independent. At their worst, they are obstinate, inhibited, and clinging. Both their chameleonlike personalities and their inability to use adult logic make them tough customers for those selling life's behavior lessons. Preschoolers live in a world that is challenging to them as well as to their parents, and teaching them—which is what disciplining really is—is sometimes like working with fertile ground and sometimes like hitting your head against a brick wall.

This should not be especially surprising. Parents and their preschoolers are usually at least twenty years apart in age and light-years apart in experience, reasoning ability, and the capacity for self-control. They also have separate ideas, feelings, expectations, rules, beliefs, and values about themselves, each other, and the world at large.

Children are not born, for example, knowing that it isn't all right to write on walls. They will only learn the desirable ways of expressing their artistic talents if their parents consistently teach them where they *can* write, praise them when they follow directions, and outline the consequences for breaking the rule.

At the same time, children have their own needs, desires, and feelings, most of which they cannot articulate very well. Throughout their first five years, they struggle to become independent human beings, and they rebel against being "raised" by older people.

The *ultimate* goals that parents have for their preschoolers are the *immediate* goals they have for themselves—self-control and self-sufficiency. When parents understand that they operate on a timetable that's different from their child's and that each child's ability to learn is different, they can lay the foundations of empathy, trust, and respect underneath the family communication.

The number one task facing parents of preschoolers is to teach them on a level they can understand how to behave appropriately in their private world at home and in public. When parents deal with their children's temper tantrums, for instance, they are not only attempting to restore calm and order to their household, they're ultimately trying to teach their children how to handle frustration and anger in a more appropriate way. And, as teachers of child discipline, parents must "model" the kind of behavior they want to teach and communicate their personal values to their children in ways that make the values as important for their offspring as they are for themselves.

PARENTHOOD IS NATURALLY PROBLEMATIC

Because childhood is naturally full of problems and conflicts, you need to ask yourself a number of questions before you label any of your child's behavior a "problem."

Ask yourself how often a certain kind of misbehavior occurs.

Then look at how intense the misbehavior is. If your child becomes angry easily, for instance, anger may be his natural reaction to disappointment. If, however, your child becomes angry with such intensity that he may injure himself or others, then you may need to give some attention to at least reducing the intensity of the anger.

Be aware of your own tolerance for your child's misbehavior.

For example, because of your own biases, needs, or rules, you may be willing to tolerate or even find amusing some behaviors that other parents find intolerable. Problems are also defined, however, by other adults. "What will the neighbors think?" moves the problem outside the family. A parent who may well accept what a child does in the home may realize that others will not approve of it and decide to do something about it.

For parents, then, a child's behavior becomes an issue or a problem from their own point of view or the point of view of others. Children do not see their tantrums as a problem, for example; they simply have not yet learned more appropriate or self-controlled ways of seeking satisfaction.

In order to manage adequately the problems of their children's behavior, parents *themselves* need to become more disciplined (where *discipline* is defined as a teaching-learning process that leads to orderliness and self-control). Parental behavior must change before a child's behavior will change, and parents must become "disciplined parents" before their children will become disciplined.

THE ABCs OF DISCIPLINED PARENTING

This section contains a summary of over twenty years of behavioral research, proving that it is important for practical as well as philosophical reasons "to separate a child from her behavior" when you deal with misbehavior problems. Calling a child who leaves her toys out a "slob" won't get the toys picked up or teach neat behavior. Its only effect on your child may be to contribute to an unhealthy self-image and possibly become a self-fulfilling prophecy. It is best for the child's self-esteem to concentrate in specific, constructive ways on changing the behavior.

Based on this principle, here are our ABCs:

Decide on the specific behavior you would like to change.
If you deal in specifics rather than abstracts, you will tend to manage better. Don't just tell your child to be "neat"; explain that you want him to pick up his blocks before he goes out to play.

Tell your child exactly what you want him to do and show him how to do it.
If you want your child to stop whining when he wants something, show him how to ask you for it. Manually guiding your children through the desired action helps them understand exactly what you want them to do.

Praise your child for doing the behavior.
Don't praise the child, but rather praise what the child is doing. An example could be saying, "It's good you're sitting quietly," rather than "You are a good boy for sitting quietly." Focus your praise or disapproval on your child's behavior because that is what you are interested in controlling.

Continue the praise as long as the new behavior needs that support.
Praising all the correct things that your children do reminds them of your expectations and continues to hold your own model of good behavior before them. If parents want to teach effectively, the best way is to exemplify what they want their children to do. Praise continues to restate the correct way of doing things.

Try to avoid power struggles with your children.
Using a technique like Beat-the-Clock (see page 7) when you want your

children to get ready for bed faster, for example, will help you reduce parent-child conflict because you transfer the authority to a neutral figure, the kitchen timer.

Be there.

This is not to say parents must be with their children every minute of every day, but it does mean that children need fairly constant supervision. If parents are there while children are playing, they can monitor the playtime, help their children learn good play habits, and bring about improvement. If they aren't paying close attention, many behavior errors will go uncorrected.

Avoid being a historian.

Leave bad behavior to history and don't keep bringing it up. If a child makes an error, constantly reminding him of his error will only lead to resentment and increase the likelihood of bad behavior. What is done is done. Working toward a better future makes more sense than dwelling on history. Reminding your children of the errors they make only holds their errors as examples of what not to do, but doesn't show them what to do. If reminding children about their errors does anything, it acts as practice in making errors.

SPANKING AND SHOUTING ARE COUNTERPRODUCTIVE

The principles outlined above represent what we as parents *should* do when we're confronted with misbehavior. What we *often* do, however, is shout at or spank our children, especially if we're tired or distracted or frustrated by their failure to obey us. Shouting and spanking are quite natural responses to misbehavior—especially continued misbehavior—but they're also quite counterproductive.

Severe punishment often generates more problems than it solves. For one thing, shouting and spanking give children all the wrong kinds of attention, and if it's the only kind we give them, they may misbehave just to get us to notice them. Also, parents don't always know if spanking works because they don't actually observe its effect over time on a child's behavior. Punishment often simply drives bad behavior underground: it stops it from happening in front of parents, but it does not stop the behavior altogether. Children, in fact, become experts at not getting caught. Parents may even say, "Don't let me catch you doing that again!"

But in the hierarchy of moral development (as defined by Lawrence Kohlberg), the lowest level is "following rules only to avoid punishment." The highest level, however, is "to follow rules because they are right and good." When we consistently spank our children for their misbehavior, we tend to stop them at the lowest level of moral development—they are interested in avoiding the punishment, not in doing what is good or right.

Spanking is also the model for the earliest experience a child has with violence. Children learn to behave in violent ways through our adult example. It is difficult to justify the admonition "Don't hit!" while parents are hitting their children for hitting. Since children see the world in concrete terms, a child who sees that it is permissible for an adult to hit a child, will assume it must then be permissible for a child to hit an adult or another child. Hitting begets hitting, as well as anger, revenge, and the breakdown of communication between parents and their children.

SELF-TALK

We encourage parents to use what we call *self-talk* in this book so that they will not fall into the habit of saying irrational things to themselves. Self-talk is best defined as what people say to themselves that governs their behavior. If, for example, a parent says, "I can't stand it when my child whines!" then his or her level of tolerance for the whining will be greatly diminished. If, however, that same parent says to him- or herself, "I don't like it when my child whines, but I can survive it," then not only will he or she be able to tolerate the whining longer, but he or she will also be likely to plan adequate ways of changing this behavior. Self-talk, then, becomes a way of setting yourself up for success rather than failure. What a person "says to himself" constitutes the most important message he'll receive, so self-talk is a great tool for parents of preschoolers. If parents can calm themselves down in times of stress by using helpful self-talk, they are more likely to follow through with reasonable and responsible actions.

USING THIS BOOK

To use this book most efficiently, think of each *do* as a remedy for a certain behavior problem. Judge for yourself the seriousness of the problem and then begin with the least severe first-aid measure. A basic rule for setting up ways of changing the behavior of children is to try the mildest strategy first. That usually involves showing your child what to do and encouraging him to do it. If that doesn't work, try the next mildest, etc., until you find something that does work. Also, since it's just as important to know what *not* to do in a behavioral crisis, try to avoid the *don'ts* listed in each section.

Doing so will help prevent behavior problems from recurring or becoming more severe.

Because parents and children are individuals, certain words and actions as they are applied in specific situations in this book will feel more natural to use for some than for others. Change a word or two if the exact language doesn't seem to come comfortably from your mouth. One- to five-year-olds are acutely aware of and sensitive to the feelings and subtle reactions of their parents. Make what you say and do believable to your child, and he will more readily accept your tactics.

A FINAL WORD

While using these remedies for successful parenting, you will be free to accept your child, because your child's behavior will be more acceptable. The remedies are also designed to show your child the kind of respect you would give others in your home. Your children learn to be respectful by being treated respectfully. Treat your child as if he were a guest in your house. That is not to say he should not follow the rules, but rather he should be made to follow the rules in a kind and respectful way.

DISCIPLINE DICTIONARY

These terms are defined here as they are used throughout this book.

Beat-the-Clock

A motivational method based on a child's competitive nature. Since children love to race to be first, by using a portable kitchen timer, parents can set up a competition between a child and time. "Can you be finished before the timer rings?" is the basic premise. Children can then race against time, with parents then being able to act as support. Beat-the-Clock has been demonstrated through research to reduce parent-child conflicts and power struggles.

Neutral Time

A time free from conflict, such as the time after a tantrum is finished and a child is calmly playing. Neutral time is the best time for teaching new behavior because it is a time of calm emotions, making children (just like adults) more receptive to learning without "static interference."

Praise

To verbally recognize a behavior you want to reinforce. Praise should always be directed toward the behavior and not toward the child. Say, "Good eating," not "Good boy for eating." Praise provides a model for statements that lead the child to a high level of moral development.

Reprimand

A sharp statement that includes the command to stop the behavior, a reason why the behavior should stop, and an alternative to the behavior, e.g., "Stop hitting; hitting hurts; ask him nicely to give you the toy."

Rule

A predetermined set of expectations with stated outcome and consequences. Establishing and enforcing rules are effective problem-solving techniques because it has been proven that children will behave more acceptably if their world is predictable and they are able to anticipate the consequences of their behavior.

Rule, Grandma's

A contractual arrangement that follows the pattern, "When you have done X, then you may do Y" (what the child wants to do). Grandma's Rule is best stated in the positive rather than the negative. It is unconditional. Never substitute the word "if" for "when." This leaves the child asking the question, "What if I don't do X?" An old-fashioned axiom was, "When you work, you eat." From this basic truism came Grandma's Rule, which has been demonstrated to have a powerful effect on behavior because it sets up established reinforcers (i.e., rewards, positive consequences) for appropriate behavior.

Time Out

To remove a person from the likelihood of any social interaction for a set period of time. A typical Time Out for children could be to sit in a chair for a specified length of time or to be put in a room for the specified period. A rule of thumb is one minute of Time Out for each year of age. When disciplining the child in this way, tell him to go to the place you have chosen, then set the timer for the specified time. If he leaves the chair before the timer rings, reset the timer, and tell him to stay in the chair until the timer rings. Repeat the process until he sits in the chair for the specified time. Research has shown that this method is an excellent alternative to more violent traditional ways of stopping such behavior, such as spanking. Why? Because Time Out has the effect of removing the child from any likelihood of receiving reinforcement (i.e., verbal attention, physical contact) or any positive consequences for inappropriate behavior during the Time Out period.

MILESTONES OF DEVELOPMENT

The chart below reveals some of the milestones that parents of normal one- to five-year-olds can expect their children to reach during their preschool years. They are general characteristics, presented at the age when they usually occur. Since every child develops on his own personal timetable, the "milestone age" may be ahead or behind the chronological age. Simply use these guidelines to educate yourself about what goes on during a particular developmental stage, keeping in mind that your child's behavior may be normal, but it may still require disciplined parenting to ensure mental and emotional well-being for him and you, as well.

Age	Milestones
1 to 2 Years	• Explores environment; gets into things • Takes one long nap a day • Plays alone for short periods of time • Explores all of his body
2 to 3 Years	• Runs, climbs, pushes, pulls; is very active • Legs appear knock-kneed • Feeds himself with fingers, spoon, cup • Can remove some of his clothing • Explores genitalia • Sleeps less, wakes easily • Likes routines • Is upset if his mother is away overnight • Wants to do things himself • Is balky and indecisive; changes his mind • Has flashes of temper and changes moods • Imitates adults • Plays beside but not with children his own age • Not yet able to share, wait, take turns, give in • Likes water play

- Prolongs "good nights"
- Uses single words, short sentences
- Is negative; says no
- Understands more than he can say

3 to 4 Years

- Runs, jumps, and climbs
- Feeds himself; drinks neatly from a cup
- Carries things without spilling
- Can help dress and undress himself
- May not sleep at naptime, but plays quietly
- Responsive to adults; wants approval
- Sensitive to expressions of disapproval
- Cooperates; likes to run simple errands
- Is at a "me too" stage; wants to be included
- Is curious about things and people
- Is imaginative; may fear dark, animals
- May have imaginary companion
- May get out of bed at night
- Is talkative; uses short sentences
- Can wait his turn; has a little patience
- Can take some responsibility (e.g., puts away toys)
- Plays well alone, but group play can be stormy
- Is attached to parent of opposite sex
- Is jealous, especially of new baby
- Gives evidence of guilt feelings
- Releases emotional insecurity by whining, crying, requesting reassurance of love
- Releases tension by thumbsucking, nail biting
- Is expressive

4 to 5 Years

- Continues to gain weight and height
- Continues to gain coordination
- Has good eating, sleeping, and elimination habits
- Is very active
- Starts things, but doesn't necessarily finish them
- Is bossy, boastful
- Plays with others, but is self-assertive
- Has short-lived quarrels
- Speaks clearly; is a great talker
- Tells stories; exaggerates
- Uses toilet words in a "silly" way
- Makes up meaningless words with lots of syllables
- Laughs, giggles
- Dawdles
- Washes when told
- "How?" and "Why?" stage
- Has a very active imagination
- Demonstrates dependence on peers

Milestones of Development

RESISTING BEDTIME

Active, energetic preschoolers who avoid sleep may turn going to bed or taking a nap into chase time, crying time, or find-another-book-to-read time to postpone the rest stop they dread. No matter what hour your child thinks is the right time to rest, stand firm to the time *you* choose. But allow your child some wind-down time to ease him gradually into the idea of turning off his motor.

Note: Since your child's need for sleep changes as he grows older, you may need to let him stay up later or shorten his nap as he ages. All children (even in the same family) do not require the same amount of sleep. (Your two-year-old may not need the same hours of rest as his older brother did when he was two.)

PREVENTING THE PROBLEM

Share a special bedtime talk.
End the day or begin a nap with a special feeling between you and your child by reciting a poem or story as a regular part of the going-to-bed routine. Make the event special so it's something your child can look forward to. Try reciting, "Night-night, sleep tight, don't let the bed bugs bite," or have a talk about the day's events, even if it's a one-sided conversation.

Make exercise a daily habit.
Make sure your child exercises his body some time during the day to help his body tell his mind not to forget going to bed.

Limit your child's naps.
Don't let your child hold off napping until nighttime and then expect him

to go to sleep an hour later. Wake him up, if necessary, to stagger asleep and awake periods.

Share prebedtime experiences.

Play with your child before you announce bedtime has come to prevent his fighting bedtime just to get your attention.

Keep bedtime consistent.

Discover how much sleep your child needs by noticing how he acts when he's taken a nap and when he hasn't, when he has gone to bed at 9:00 P.M. and at 7:00 P.M. Then establish the same sleep schedule to fit his time clock.

SOLVING THE PROBLEM

WHAT TO DO

Play Beat-the-Clock.

Here's how it works: An hour before bedtime (or naptime), set the timer for five minutes. This allows your child to anticipate the upcoming events. When the timer rings, reset it for about fifteen minutes, during which time you and your child (or him alone, if he's capable) get ready for bed (take a bath, get into pajamas, brush teeth, get a drink, go to the bathroom, etc.). If your child beats the timer, he gets to stay up and play for the remaining forty minutes of the hour. If he doesn't beat the clock, don't take away any privileges; just put him in bed.

Use the bedtime routine regardless of time.

Even if bedtime has been delayed for some reason, go through the same rituals to help your child learn what's expected of him when it comes to going to bed. Don't point out how late he's stayed up. Quicken the pace by helping him with the rituals of getting into pajamas or getting a drink, for example, and set the timer for thirty minutes in the beginning, instead of sixty; but don't omit any steps.

Mind the order.

Since preschoolers find comfort in consistency, have him bathe, brush his teeth, and put on his pajamas in the same order every night. Ask your child to name what step in the routine comes next to make a game out of getting ready for bed, with your child calling the shots.

Offer rewards for beating the clock.

Greet your child upon waking with the good news that beating the clock is worth its while. Say, "You did so well getting in bed that I'll fix you your favorite breakfast" or "Because you got in bed so nicely I'll read you a story now."

Don't let your child control bedtime.

Stick with your chosen bedtime despite your child's resistance or attempts to delay it. Remember that you know why your child doesn't want to go to bed—and why he should. Say to yourself, "He's only crying because he doesn't want to end his playtime, but I know he'll play happier later if he sleeps now."

Don't threaten or spank.

Threatening or spanking your child to get him into bed can cause nightmares and fears, besides making you feel upset and guilty because the behavior persists. Use the timer as a neutral authority to determine when bedtime arrives to take the blame off you.

Don't remind your child of his restless nature.

Don't make him pay for resisting sleep after he's gotten up. Repeat the Beat-the-Clock game until he plays it naturally.

BEDTIME AT SAM'S

Evenings at the Shores' house meant one thing—a tearful battle of wills between three-year-old Sam and his father when the younger Shore's bedtime was announced.

"I'm not tired! I don't want to go to bed! I want to stay up!" Sam pleaded each night as his angry father dragged him to bed. "I know you don't want to go to bed," his father said, "but you will do what I say, and I say it's bedtime!"

Forcing his son to bed upset Mr. Shore as much as it did his little boy. Even though *he* believed that he should be boss, he knew that their fights kept Sam crying in his pillow and him trying to figure out how to make going to bed less stressful.

The next night Mr. Shore decided to control himself and let something else, the kitchen timer, control bedtime. An hour before Sam's bedtime, he set the timer for five minutes. "It's time to start getting ready for bed," Mr. Shore explained to his curious son. "If you get yourself ready for bed before the timer rings, we'll set the timer again and you can stay up for the rest of the hour and play. If you don't beat the timer, you must go to bed right away and there will be no more playing until morning."

Sam raced around and got ready for bed before the timer rang. As promised, Mr. Shore reset the timer, then read Sam his favorite animal tales and sang some new sleepytime songs until the timer rang again almost an hour later. "It's time for bed, right?" Sam announced, acting delighted to have this game all figured out. "That's right! You're so smart!" said his dad.

As the two journeyed up to bed, Mr. Shore once again told his son how proud he was of his "beating the clock." The incentives and consequences Sam's dad shared with his son helped them enjoy a warless evening for the first time in months. After several weeks of following this routine, going to bed never became something to look forward to, but it was far from a struggle for Sam and his dad.

GETTING OUT OF BED AT NIGHT

Children under six are famous for piping up with requests for books, kisses, or getting in bed with their parents immediately after mom and dad leave their bedside or the lights are out. Remember that your child's nightly need is for sleep, though she may want ten books and four drinks just to see what you're up to or to have you near her again. Teach your child that going to sleep will bring you back to her bedside faster than demanding attention.

Note: If you don't know whether it's a need or a want your child is expressing (if your child is not yet talking or simply cries out instead of saying what she wants), go check on her. If all is medically sound, give her a quick kiss and hug (thirty seconds maximum) and make your exit. Tell her firmly and lovingly that it's time for sleep, not play.

PREVENTING THE PROBLEM

Discuss bedtime rules at a nonbedtime time.

Set limits for how many drinks of water or trips to the toilet your child may have at bedtime. Tell her these rules at a neutral time so she is aware of what you expect her to do when bedtime comes. Say, "You can take two books to bed and have one drink, and I'll tell you two stories before you hit the sack." If your child likes to get in bed with you, decide before she arrives whether your rules allow that. (No evidence exists to support whether it is good or harmful for children to be in the same bed with their parents.)

Promise rewards for following the rules.

Make your child aware that following rules, not breaking them, will bring her bonuses. Say, "When you've stayed in your own bed all night (if that's your rule), then you may have Cheerios for breakfast." Rewards could include special breakfasts, trips to the park, games, playtime with you, or anything you know is enjoyable for your child.

Plant the idea of going back to sleep.

Remind your child of the rules as you put her in bed, to strengthen her memory about previous discussions.

SOLVING THE PROBLEM

WHAT TO DO

Help your child follow the rules.

Make breaking the rules more trouble than it's worth. When your child breaks a rule by asking for more than two drinks, for example, go to her bedside and say, "I'm sorry you got out of bed and broke the two-drink rule. Now you must have your door closed, as we said" (if that's what you said you would do if she asked for more drinks of water).

Stand firm with your rules.

Enforce the rule every time your child breaks it, to teach her that you mean what you say. For example, when you put your child back in bed after she gets into bed with you in violation of your rule, say, "I'm sorry that you got in bed with us. Remember the rule; everyone sleeps in her own bed. I love you. See you in the morning."

Follow through with rewards.

Make sure your child trusts you by always making good on your reward for following the rules.

WHAT NOT TO DO

Don't go back on your promise.

Once you've set the rules, don't change them unless you discuss this first with your child. Every time you don't enforce the rules, your child only learns to keep trying to get what she wants, even though you've said no.

Don't give in to noise.

If your child screams because you enforced the rule, remember she's learning something that is important for her own health—night is for sleeping. Time how long your child cries, to see the progress you are making in getting her not to resist sleep. If you don't respond to the noise, it should gradually decrease in duration until it disappears completely.

Don't use threats and fear.

Threats such as "If you get out of bed, the lizards will get you," or "If you do that one more time, I'm going to whip you," will only increase the

Getting Out of Bed at Night

problem because, unless you back them up, threats are only noise without meaning. Fear may keep your child in bed, but the fear may generalize until your child becomes afraid of many things.

Don't talk to your child from a distance.

Yelling threats and rules out of your child's sight teaches her to yell and lets her know that you don't care enough to talk to her face-to-face.

JENNIFER'S MIDNIGHT RAMBLINGS

Two-and-a-half-year-old Jennifer Long had been sleeping through the night without waking until dawn since she was six months old. For the past month, however, she stayed asleep for only a few hours before waking up her slumbering parents around midnight with screams of "Mommy! Daddy!"

At first, Jennifer's mom or dad would race up to see what was wrong with their daughter, only to find her begging for drinks of water one night, an extra hug the next, and bathroom visits on other evenings.

After several weeks of these interruptions, Jennifer's weary parents decided to get serious and put a stop to these requests. "If you don't stay in bed, you're going to be punished, young lady," they commanded, then returned to their bed, only to hear their daughter padding down the stairs toward their room. They tried spanking Jennifer firmly and telling her to "Get in bed or else!" but their heavy hand seemed to carry little weight.

The Longs kept telling themselves that Jennifer's waking up in the middle of the night was natural—everyone went through shallow and deep sleep periods. But they also knew that their daughter *could* choose to go back to sleep instead of calling out to them.

To solve the problem, they planned to offer Jennifer more attention for staying in bed. "If you stay in bed without calling out to us," they explained as they tucked her in her bed the next night, "you will have your favorite surprise at breakfast in the morning. If you call out in the middle of the night, we will close your door, you will have to stay in bed, and you will have no surprise." They made sure they stated the new rule in plain, three-year-old terms.

That night, Jennifer still called out for her mother. "I want a drink!" But her mother followed through with her promise to close her door and not answer her cries. "I'm sorry you didn't go back to sleep, Jennifer. Now we'll have to close your door. I'll see you in the morning."

After three nights of closed doors and interrupted sleep for all the Longs, Jennifer learned that calling out did not bring her parents to her bedside and that staying quiet and in bed all night made the promised surprises materialize in the morning. And not only were her parents more well-rested, but Jennifer found that the praise for sleeping through the night made her feel grown-up and important—two extra rewards.

NOT EATING

Though parents have been pushing their on-the-go preschoolers to eat since the beginning of parenthood, many modern children under six are still too busy investigating their world to take much time out for chewing. If the temptation to force food on your child seems nearly inborn, try to give him more attention for eating (even the smallest pea!) than for not eating.

Note: Don't mistake typical, occasional noneating behavior for illness. Get professional help if you feel your child is physically ill and can't eat.

PREVENTING THE PROBLEM

Don't skip meals yourself.
Skipping meals yourself gives your child the idea that not eating is okay for him, since it's okay for you.

Don't emphasize a big tummy or idolize a bone-thin physique.
Even a three-year-old can become irrationally weight-conscious if you show him how to be obsessed with his body fat.

Learn the appropriate amount of food for your child's age and weight.
Understand what normal levels of eating are for your child, so that your expectations will be realistic. (See Appendix 2, page 133.)

Create eating-time schedules.
Get your child's system in the habit of needing nourishment at a particular time, and his body will tell him that it needs food then.

Solving the Problem

Encourage less food, more often.

Your child's stomach isn't as large as yours, so it often can't hold enough to last three to four hours between meals. Let your child eat as often as he likes, but only the right foods for good nutrition. Say, "Whenever you're hungry, let me know, and you can have celery with peanut butter or an apple with cheese," for example. Make sure you want to follow through with your suggestions, based on what foods are in the house and what time a bigger meal is coming.

Let your child choose foods.

Let your child decide (sometimes) what between-meal snack or lunch foods he wants (with your supervision). If he feels that he has some control over what he's eating, he may be more excited about food. Praise wise choices (only give two, so he is not overwhelmed with the decision-making process) with comments like, "I'm really glad you chose that orange; it's really a delicious snack."

Provide variety and balance.

Children need to learn about proper diet. Play teacher by offering a range of tastes, textures, colors, and aromas of nutritious foods. Remember that preschoolers' tastes seem to change overnight, so expect your child to turn down a food today that was a favorite last week.

Let nature take its course.

A normal, healthy child will naturally select a balanced diet over a week's time, which pediatricians say will adequately nourish him. Keep a mental note of what your child has eaten from Monday through Sunday, not from sunup to sundown, before becoming alarmed that he's undernourished.

Catch your child with a mouthful.

Give your child encouragement when he downs a spoonful of anything—to teach him that eating will bring him as much attention as not eating. Praise good eating habits by saying, "That's great the way you put that meat loaf in your mouth all by yourself," or "I'm glad you like the rolls we have today."

Make mealtime eating time.

Because they are not on the same eating schedule as you, children often want to play outside or finish block building just when a mealtime arrives. They may need to be trained to switch to your time clock for sitting together, at least. Do this *not* by forcing your child to eat a lot of food, but by setting a timer for the length of time he must remain at the table, eating or not. Say, "The timer will tell us when dinner is over. The rule is that you must stay at the table until the timer rings. Tell me when you're done eating and I'll remove your plate." Let children under three stay at the table a shorter time than a four- or five-year-old, who will have a longer attention span. Keep in mind when your child seems to get hungry to learn what kind of hunger clock he's on—which you could switch to, if possible.

WHAT NOT TO DO

Don't always offer a food reward for eating.

Keep food in perspective. Food is meant to provide nourishment, not symbolize praise. Say, "Since you ate your green beans so nicely, you can go outside after dinner."

Don't bribe or beg.

When your child is not eating, don't bribe or beg him to clean his plate. This makes noneating a game to get your attention and gives your child a feeling of power over you.

Don't get upset when your child won't eat.

Giving him attention for not eating makes not eating much more satisfying for your child than eating.

Don't talk about your child's noneating with others.

Keep the attention you give to your child's eating patterns in perspective, so food will not be the battleground where you wage power struggles.

"I WON'T EAT!"

When John Rowland turned four years old, his appetite dropped to zero. His parents didn't know why and neither did his pediatrician who checked him over physically at the insistence of John's fretful mother.

One night after Mrs. Rowland had begged him to eat just "one pea," John threw a vehement tantrum, pushed his plate off the table, and shouted, "No, I won't eat!"

Mr. Rowland decided he had let his wife handle the situation for too long. "Now, Johnny, listen to me. If you don't take a bite of that maca-roni, you'll have to leave the table," he threatened, firmly letting his son know the rule of the moment and never guessing that Johnny would take him up on the invitation and get down from his chair.

"Johnny Rowland, you will *not* get down from this table! You will stay and eat your dinner if you have to sit here all night!" Mr. Rowland ruled, changing the orders and thoroughly confusing his son.

Later that night, after they had kissed and hugged their son and put him to bed, the Rowlands decided that something else must be done—they were starting to spank and yell at their little boy. They wanted to turn mealtime back into what it used to be—a time for food and fun exchanges of stories, songs, and tales of the day's events.

The next night at dinner, they shifted their attention away from food and pretended to ignore John's lack of appetite. "Tell me about how you were the helper at preschool today," Johnny's mother began with all the sincerity and calmness she could muster, as she passed the broccoli to her husband. John perked up as he told the story of how he was chosen to hold the flag, and he just happened to swallow a forkful of mashed potatoes in between his excited explanation.

"That was so nice of you to be such a good helper today," Mrs. Rowland complimented her son. "I'm glad you like the mashed potatoes, too," she added. The Rowlands continued their meal but refrained from pushing their son to "try a few more potatoes."

The next morning John's parents discussed the evening's success and decided to continue what they were doing and also put one suggestion of John's doctor into practice. "John may only eat small amounts, judging from his normal but slight body size, and he may eat those more than three times a day, as many people do," the doctor had said. So dinnertime became less of a daytime preoccupation for Mrs. Rowland. She began creating fun carrot stick boats and cheese and raisin faces for snacks; Johnny developed a whole new interest in eating more during the day, though he still only took a few minutes to swallow his dinner. But the Rowlands appreciated those minutes John *did* spend eating, and they let their son dictate when he was and wasn't hungry.

PLAYING WITH FOOD

Take a one-, two-, or three-year-old, mix her with food she doesn't want to eat, and her parents have a mess on their hands, their child's hands, and undoubtedly on the floor and table, too. When your child's hunger doesn't get food to her mouth, her playfully fingering it tells you she has eaten all she wants, whether she can actually say the words or not. Consistently take your child's food away as soon as it becomes a weapon or piece of clay to teach her that food is to be eaten or it won't be there—even if she's still hungry.

PREVENTING THE PROBLEM

Don't play with food yourself.
If you flip peas with your fork, even unconsciously, your child will assume that's what she can do, too.

Plan food your child likes to eat (at least one at each meal) and can eat.
Make bite-size pieces that are easily edible. To minimize the amount of work she'll have to do to get food in her mouth, cut her food and butter her roll before setting her plate in front of her.

Keep bowls of food off the table.
Steer playful preschoolers away from the temptation to stir and pour just for fun.

Teach your child table rules (at a noneating, neutral time).
Your child needs to know what you expect of her in restaurants and at home because she doesn't have built-in manners. Have frequent tea parties, for instance, where you show her how to use her spoon, keep food on the table, keep her hands out of the food, tell you when she's done, etc. For example, tell your child under two, "Say 'I'm done' and

then you can get down and play." Tell your three-, four-, or five-year-old, "When the timer rings, you can leave the table. Tell me when you're finished and I'll take your plate."

Talk to your child at the table.

If you try to make conversation with her, she won't find other ways to get your attention, like playing with food.

SOLVING THE PROBLEM

WHAT TO DO

Compliment proper eating habits.

Any time your child is not playing with food at the table, tell her you like how well she's eating, to drive home the point that she will be rewarded for eating nicely. Say, for example, "That's great the way you're using your fork for those peas," or "Thanks for twisting that spaghetti around your fork as I showed you."

Make playing with food unappetizing.

If your child breaks an eating rule you've previously discussed, tell her what the consequences are, to prove to her that playing with food will cost her some pleasurable time. Say, "I'm sorry that you stuck your hands into your mashed potatoes. Now dinner is over. You will have to clean up the mess," for example.

Ask whether your child is done when she starts to play with food.

Don't immediately assume that your child is being devilish. Ask her why she's dissecting her meat loaf to give her a chance to explain herself (if she is verbal).

WHAT NOT TO DO

Don't lose your cool.

Though you may be disgusted and angry at your child for wasting food by playing with it, your anger may be the spice that your child wants with her meal. Your preschooler thrives on having the power to affect the world (for better and worse). Don't let playing with food become a way to get attention. Ignore any nondestructive food play that you feel comfortable accepting at the table.

Don't give in.

If your child has to pay the price for playing with food, don't give in and remove the cost, even if she's screaming about how high it is. Teach your child you mean what you say every time you make a deal with her.

DINNERTIME DISASTERS

Dinnertime at the Langners' looked more like art class than mealtime, since three-year-old Nick had begun smearing food around his plate and spitting out what didn't tickle his taste buds.

His parents, who were disgusted with their son's wasteful games, tried to stop him by screaming, "Don't play with your food!" each time Nick began his fun. Even after his mother threatened, "If you do that with your peas one more time, I'll take you down from the table," Nick tried to flip one more pea into his glass of milk.

Spanking didn't bring any results either—Nick continued to eat only a few bites and then started feeding his frankfurters and beans to the nearby plants.

So the Langners began to anticipate just when Nick might be full and then removed the plate when his playful eyes and hands started to find new things to do with french fries and green beans. Nick's mother also spent a few minutes during the day teaching her son the words "Through now," which he could use to signal when he was done eating.

Both Nick's parents were relieved that they had gone through three weeks without any food art at the table when Nick began smearing creamed corn on the tablecloth. But they had decided what the rule would be for "slip ups," and they explained it calmly to Nick.

"Now that you have made this mess, you must clean it up, too," they informed him and then demonstrated the process, instead of yelling at him. Nick didn't get any attention for having to clean up his mess by himself and it took only three wipe-up nights for him to begin to start saying, "Through now," instead of creating a disaster area around him. Those words worked magic, he discovered, because he appreciated the hugs and kisses from his parents, who would say, "Thanks for saying 'through now,' Nick. I know you're done with your dinner and now you may go play with your trucks while we finish ours."

The whole family seemed relieved that more time was spent talking about how nice Nick was eating instead of how destructive he was with his food. Dinners with their son were shorter but sweeter than ever before.

OVEREATING

The appetite of many children under six can be as endless as that of the famous Cookie Monster on TV. Like that puppet hero, your child is not aware of why he wants more food than he needs. But *you* need to be in order to get his eating habits back on the right track. Because overeating is a symptom of a problem, not the problem itself, try to discover the reasons behind your child's seemingly bottomless pit. For example, see if he overeats out of habit, boredom, mimicry, or the desire for attention. Help him satisfy his wants without eating, just as you would yourself.

Note: Get professional help if your child is a consistent overeater. Avoid nonmedically supervised diets.

PREVENTING THE PROBLEM

Become well versed in what's appropriate for your child.
Before you dictate an eating plan, learn the normal amount for your child to eat and the average weight for his size and sex. (See Appendix 2, page 133.)

Serve healthy foods.
Keep high-calorie, empty-calorie foods out of your overeater's reach so he won't be tempted to grab for them.

Check your child's diet.
Since your preschooler is too young to decide what he can and can't have, it's up to you to establish nutritious eating habits, the younger the better. Foods high in fat and sugar should be replaced with those high in protein, to offer a balance of nutritious calories and nutrition in a day.

Teach when, how, and where eating is allowed.

Restrict eating to the kitchen and dining room only. Slow down the eating pace and insist that food be eaten from a plate or bowl, instead of directly from the refrigerator. More rest between mouthfuls is a proven way to get the message to our brains that we are full before we've eaten more than we need (it takes twenty minutes for the process to work).

SOLVING THE PROBLEM

WHAT TO DO

Provide pleasurable activities other than eating.

Get to know what your child likes to do besides eat, and suggest it after you know he's eaten enough to satisfy his hunger—showing him how "delicious" things other than eating can be.

Keep food in perspective.

Don't always offer food as a present or reward, to avoid teaching your child that food holds meaning other than to satisfy hunger.

Stagger mealtimes so your child doesn't get over-hungry and gorge on food when it finally arrives.

Watch when your child overeats.

Try to discover why your child overeats by seeing if he turns to food when he's bored, sees others gorge on food, is mad, sad, wants attention from you, or has gotten into the habit. Then resolve these feelings in other noneating ways, like talking or playing. Communicate about trouble spots in your child's life so that food won't be a problem-solver.

Practice control yourself.

It's been documented that the father models the eating pattern that children seem to pick up the quickest. If parents snack and eat empty-calorie junk foods all day, their children will feel that it's okay to do that themselves.

Praise wise food selections.

You can mold preferences just by your tone and by encouraging foods you want to become favorites. Whenever your child picks up an orange instead of a piece of chocolate for a snack, say "That's a great choice you made for something to eat. I'm glad you're taking care of yourself so well by eating yummy treats like oranges."

Encourage your child to exercise.

Overweight children often don't eat any more than normal-weight children; they just don't burn enough calories off through exercise. Suggest physical games to play in the winter, like dancing or jumping rope. In the summer, swimming, walking, baseball, and swinging are not only good for your child's physical development, but they also relieve tension, give him fresh air, and build coordination and strength. Your participation in the exercise, no matter what form, will make it seem like a game instead of grueling work.

Communicate with your child.

Make sure that your encouraging your child to eat all his peas isn't the only encouragement you ever give him. Praise his artwork, the clothes he's chosen, and the way he cleaned up his toys, as well as the job he did cleaning his plate, to let your child see that he gets attention for things other than eating and overeating.

WHAT NOT TO DO

Don't give in to his food wants.

Just because your child wants to eat more doesn't mean he needs to, but don't make him feel guilty for wanting more. Briefly explain why he should not have more, because your child is too young to tell himself the reason.

Don't give treats only when your child is upset.

Your child may build all the wrong associations with food if you consistently offer it to ease his pain.

Don't consistently allow food when you're watching TV.

Because television advertising bombards your child with food messages, help him get away from constantly concerning himself with food by limiting television viewing.

Don't give junk foods as snacks.

What you allow for snacks and meals is what your child will expect. Food preferences are often habits, not inborn.

Don't make fun of your child if he's overweight.

Making fun of your child only compounds the problem by adding to his guilt and shame.

"NO MORE COOKIES!"

Two-and-a-half-year-old Audry Hanlon was getting a reputation at preschool and family functions for being a "walking bottomless pit." If food was in sight, Audry ate it. She never seemed to be full.

"No, you cannot have another cookie, Audry!" Mrs. Hanlon would scream at her daughter every time she caught her with a hand in the cookie jar. "You've had enough cookies to last your lifetime!" she added one day. But neither angry outbursts nor the threat of taking her tricycle away lessened Audry's desire to finish every morsel in a box or on a plate.

A checkup by her pediatrician helped Mrs. Hanlon learn how to change Audry's eating habits. Audry asked for another helping of oatmeal the day after the doctor had given Mrs. Hanlon a diet plan and recipe suggestions. Mrs. Hanlon finally had an answer for her daughter that wasn't angry or insulting: "I'm glad you like the oatmeal, Audry. We can have some more tomorrow morning. Let's go read that new book now," she suggested. Knowing that the amount she had given Audry was nutritionally adequate for her made it easier for Mrs. Hanlon to stand firm when Audry begged for more of her favorite cereal. It also made it easier for her to plan each meal, knowing that she may simply be depriving her daughter of something she wanted, not needed.

For the next month, the Hanlons didn't allow an unlimited supply of cookies, so Audry started to try new foods that were freely given and colorful and more filling. "That's great the way you picked an orange for a snack instead of the cookies," Mrs. Hanlon said, realizing that any time Audry chose a nutritious food item she should be rewarded with praise.

Audry started to hear fewer comments about being a bottomless pit and received lots of hugs and compliments for eating fruit not fudge—compliments that encouraged her to eat nutritionally for the first time. Not only were her parents more delighted to share exercise and fun with her, but Audry seemed to be more fun for her friends and teachers, too.

OVERUSING NO

No ranks as the most-likely-to-be-used word by one- to three-year-olds because it's the most-likely-to-be-used word by their parents. Toddlers are famous for getting into, on top of, and underneath things, making parents famous for saying, "No! Don't touch!" "No! Don't open!" "No! Don't do that!" To see what and who they can control, two- and three-year-olds throw a no right back whenever tossed a yes-no question. Limit the opportunities you give your child to say no (avoid asking yes-no questions) and don't always take her literally when she says no to every request.

PREVENTING THE PROBLEM

Get to know your child's personality.

If you're familiar with your child's wants and desires, you'll know when her no really means yes or when she really *doesn't* want something.

Think before saying no.

Avoid telling your child no when you don't really care if she does something or not.

Limit yes-no questions.

Don't ask questions that could be answered with a no. Ask how much juice she wants, for example, instead of whether she wants some juice. If you want her to get in the car, don't say, "Do you want to get into the car?" Say, "We're getting in the car now," and do it!

Change your own no to something different.

For example, say "stop" instead of no when your child does something you don't want her to, like touch the plants.

Get your child to stop a behavior by teaching her to do something else.
Because you usually want your child to stop a behavior when you say no to her, teach another behavior to replace the one you want stopped. During a neutral time, take your child's hand, say, "Come here, please!" and draw her to you. Give her a hug and say, "Thank you for coming." Practice five times a day, slowly increasing the distance your child is away from you when you say "Come here, please" until she can come to you from across the room or across the shopping center.

SOLVING THE PROBLEM

WHAT TO DO

Ignore your child's no.
Take the positive side and assume she really means yes. If she really doesn't want the juice she just said no to, for example, she won't take it. Soon you'll know if she's crying wolf or not when she says no.

Give more attention for yes than no.
Your child will soon learn how to say yes if nodding her head positively or saying yes makes you smile and give her praise. React to that word positively by saying something like, "How nice that you said yes" or "I'm really glad you said yes when your aunt asked you that question."

Teach how to say yes.
Children over three can learn to say yes if they're methodically shown. Try this plan: Tell your child that you want to hear her say yes. Next, praise her for saying it with words like, "It's nice to hear you saying yes" or "I really like the way you said yes." Then say, "I'm going to ask you to do something for me and I want you to say yes before I can count to five." If she says it, tell her what a great yes that was. Practice this five times for five days and you'll be in for a more positive-sounding child.

Let your child say no.
Even though she must still do what you want her to do or need her to do, your child is entitled to say no. When you want your child to do something, but she has said no, explain the situation to your child. For example, say, "I know you don't want to pick up your crayons, but when you have done what I asked, then you may do what you want to." This lets your child know that you hear her express her feelings and take those into consideration—but you're still the boss.

Don't laugh or encourage the use of no.
Laughing or calling attention to your child's overuse of no only encourages her to use it more to get your response.

Don't get angry.
Remember that the no stage is normal in your developing preschooler and will soon pass. Getting angry will be interpreted as giving your child attention for saying no, and attention and power are just what she wants.

NEGATIVE NATHAN

Twenty-month-old Nathan Shelb's favorite word to say— no—was his parents' least favorite word to hear. Because little Nate used that word to answer every question asked of him, his parents started to wonder about his mental powers. "Can't you say *anything* besides no?" they'd ask their son, only to get his usual response.

So the Shelbs tried to reduce the number of times *they* used the word no during the day, to see if it would have any effect on Nathan's vocabulary. Instead of just saying, "No, not now," whenever Nate demanded a cookie, they said, "Yes, you may have a cookie when you have eaten dinner."

While they were still in effect saying no, Nate didn't react negatively in return—he took his parents up on their promise and *did* get his cookie immediately after dinner.

As his parents traded in their no's for yes's, Nate started to increase his use of yes, a word that was immediately met with smiles, hugs, and compliments from his delighted parents. "Thanks for saying yes when I asked you if you wanted to take a bath," his mother would say. They were delighted that their son was decreasing his no's in direct proportion to how much praise he got for saying yes.

The Shelbs also tried to limit the number of yes-no questions they asked Nate. Instead of asking him *if* he wanted something to drink with his dinner, they would say, "Do you want apple juice or milk, Nathan?" and Nathan would happily make a choice between the two. Their efforts were painless ways to control their son's negativism, and they soon found their household taking on a more positive note.

TEMPER TANTRUMS

Millions of normal, lovable preschoolers throw temper tantrums as their violent, emotional way of coping with frustration or anger and telling the world they're the boss. The cure? Tantrums can become less frequent and be prevented without giving the performer an audience and giving in to his wants. Though you may want to give in or crawl under the nearest checkout counter when your child throws a tantrum in public, be patient until he's done and praise his gaining control after he's calm.

Note: Common, periodic crying is not a temper tantrum and needs to be treated in a different way. Get professional help if your child has more than two to three temper tantrums per day.

PREVENTING THE PROBLEM

Teach your child how to handle frustration and anger.

Show your child how adults like you can find other ways of coping besides yelling and screaming. When you burn the casserole, for instance, instead of throwing the burned pot into the garbage, say, "I'm upset now, honey, but I can handle it. I'm going to figure out how to solve this mess by seeing what else I can fix for dinner." Regardless of the situation, teach your child to look at the choices he has to solve his problems instead of getting violent about them.

Give pats on the back.

Try to catch your child being good. For instance, when he asks you to help him make a complicated puzzle work, praise him. Say, "I'm so glad you asked for my help, instead of getting mad at the puzzle." Helping your child to handle his own frustration and anger calmly helps him feel good about himself. You'll find him repeating a calm problem-solving technique when he knows he'll get praised for it. Tell him you understand that he's frustrated, though, by saying, "I know how you feel when things get tough, and I'm really proud of you for being able to take it."

Don't let playtime always mean alone time.

Knowing that being good means that mom or dad goes away increases the chances that your child will be bad just to get you back into his play picture.

Don't wait for an invitation.

If you spot some trouble brewing in your child's play and eating activities, for example, don't let it simmer too long. When you see that the situation is one he can't control or make easier, say, "I bet this puzzle piece goes here" or "Let's do it this way." Show him how to work the toy or eat the food, and then let *him* complete the task so he feels good about his ability to let others help.

SOLVING THE PROBLEM

WHAT TO DO

Ignore your child's tantrum.

Do nothing for, with, or to your child during his performance. Teach him that a temper tantrum is not the way to get your attention and not the way to get his wants attended to. But how do you ignore a tornado tearing through your living room? Walk away from him during his tantrum, turn your back on him, put him in his room, or isolate yourself. If he's being destructive or dangerous to himself or others in public, put him in the car or some other confined place. Don't even look his way during this isolation. Though it's tough to turn away, try to busy yourself in another room of the house or with another activity in public.

Try to stand firm.

Despite the power of your child's screaming and pounding, make sure you've got power over the situation by holding tight to your rule about the matter. Tell yourself silently that it's important for your child to learn he can't have everything he wants when he wants it. Your child is learning to be realistic and you are learning to be consistent and to give him boundaries for acceptable and unacceptable behavior.

Remain as calm as you can.

Say to yourself, "This is not a big deal. I can control my child while teaching him to control himself. He's just trying to get me upset so he can have what he wants." Keeping calm while ignoring your child is the best model for him when he's upset. So go about your business.

Praise your child.

After the fire of a temper tantrum is just smoldering, immediately praise your child for gaining self-control and then get both of you into a favorite game or activity that is not frustrating for him or you. Say "I'm glad you're feeling better now. I love you, but I don't like screaming or yelling." Since this is your only reference to the tantrum, it will help him know that it was the tantrum you were ignoring, not him.

Explain rule changes.

If you and your child are at the dime store and he asks to buy a toy car that was off-limits for him before, you can change your mind—but change your message too. Say, "Remember when we were last here and you threw a tantrum? If you behave nicely by staying close to me, I've decided that you can have the car." This will help him understand that it wasn't the tantrum that changed your mind; you're buying the car for another reason. If you like, tell him the reasons you changed your mind, particularly if they include praise for good behavior.

WHAT NOT TO DO

Don't reason or explain.

Trying to reason or talk your child out of his tantrum *during* the tantrum is wasted breath. He doesn't care—he's in the middle of a show and he's a star! Any discussion now only encourages the tantrum because it gives him the audience he wants.

Don't throw a tantrum yourself.

Say to yourself, "Why do I need to act crazy? I know that when I said no, I said it for a reason." Losing your cool will only encourage your child to keep the heat on.

Don't belittle your child.

Just because your child had a temper tantrum doesn't mean he's a bad person. Don't say, "Bad boy! Aren't you ashamed of yourself?" Your child will lose respect for himself and feel that he didn't deserve what he wanted anyway.

Don't be a historian.

Don't remind your child of his tantrum later that day. This only gives more attention to the behavior and increases the chances he'll have a tantrum again, just to be the center of your conversation.

Don't make your child pay for the tantrum.

Having nothing to do with him *after* it's over will only cause him to have more tantrums to try to get your attention. Don't make him feel unloved and unwanted just because his behavior was.

TANTRUM TIME

Donald and Mary MacLean were worried about their two-year-old, Amy, who got a bad attack of "temper tantrumitis" every time her request for a cookie before dinner was refused. When her parents said no, she would scream yes, pull on her father's pant leg, and jump up and down on the kitchen floor, until both she and her distraught parents were so exhausted that they finally gave in.

In frustration, the MacLeans wondered what they were doing wrong. Was there something terribly wrong with saying no to Amy's demands? What finally occurred to them was that Amy's tantrums were more frequent when they said no to her. They also realized that giving in to Amy's uncontrollable desire for a cookie before dinner only encouraged her bad behavior.

The next time Amy had a tantrum, they were ready with a new strategy. When the tantrum exploded, instead of saying no, Mary said, matter-of-factly, "Amy, I know you want the cookie, but you will not get it until you are first quiet and then have finished your dinner."

Amy didn't stop her tantrum, but her parents simply walked away from their mad child, leaving her with no audience for her big scene. Though it was hard to keep from peeking in on their tantruming child, the MacLeans waited until their daughter was quiet before entering the kitchen again. Without any physical or verbal attention, Amy had stopped wailing and was waiting to see if her parents would practice what they preached.

When she stopped screaming, her father appeared, wearing a smile, and said, "Amy, I know you want that cookie now, but when you have eaten your dinner and we are ready for dessert, you may certainly have the cookie. I'm glad you're not screaming and yelling now. It's nice to see you control yourself." Amy quietly went to dinner and, as promised, when she finished eating, her parents brought her a cookie.

The MacLeans complimented themselves that night on the self-control *they* had exhibited in not giving in and giving Amy's tantrum an audience. Though they were tempted later to give in again, they continued to remove themselves from their daughter when she had a tantrum, as well as to praise her any time she reacted peacefully when something was denied her. The frequency of Amy's tantrums diminished to the point that Amy would cry from time to time when she was disappointed, but she wouldn't have the reckless scenes she often had in the past.

WHINING

Just as adults often find themselves in a bad mood for no reason, nearly every little adult sometimes seems to have no reason for whining and crankiness. If you know all your child's needs are met (she's dry, fed, etc.), the reason behind your preschooler's feeling and acting out of sorts is her wanting attention or her own way. Though it's hard to do, ignoring a moaner does help wind down the whining. Your child will soon learn an important home rule—asking nicely speaks louder than being cranky and noncommunicative.

PREVENTING THE PROBLEM

Catch 'em being good.

Praise any good behavior and any successful attempts at doing things right to prevent your child from whining and moaning about how "nothing she does is right."

Keep her needs met.

Make sure your child eats, bathes, dresses, sleeps, and gets plenty of hugs as regularly (for her) as possible to prevent her becoming cranky because she's uncomfortable and too upset about a situation to tell you her feelings without crying.

SOLVING THE PROBLEM

WHAT TO DO

Teach what whining is and isn't.

Make sure your child knows exactly what you mean by the word "whine" when you ask her to please not whine. Then explain how you'd like her to ask for something or tell you what she wants without whining about it. Say, for example, "I will not give you apple juice until you ask nicely. Here's how I'd like you to ask for some apple juice: 'Mommy (or Daddy), may I please have some apple juice to drink?' " If she's in the pretalking stage, show your child how to point to or take you to what she wants with actions, not words. Let her practice requesting things pleasantly at least five times, followed by your fulfilling the request to prove your point.

Create a whining and crying place.

If your child's whining continues even after you've taught her how to express her wants nicely, let her know that she has the right to have feelings and frustrations that only crying might relieve. Tell her that she can cry and whine as much as she wants, but that she must do it in the "crying place," a place you designate only for crying. Let her know that you'd rather not be around a whiner and cryer who can't tell you what she wants, and when she's done crying she can come out. Say, for example, "I'm sorry you are so upset. You can go to the crying place and come back when you feel better."

Ignore your child's whining.

Because your child's whining is so nerve-racking, you can easily pay more attention to her when she whines than when she's quiet, even though that attention is not affection. Wear headphones if the whining gets above tolerance level, after you've put her in the whining chair and given her the go-ahead to get the frustration or bad day out of her system.

Point out nonwhining times.

To show your child the vivid contrast between how you react when she does and doesn't whine, immediately praise her quieting down by saying, "You are being so pleasant, let's go get a toy!" or "I haven't heard you cry for the longest time!" or "Thanks for not whining."

WHAT NOT TO DO

Don't give in to a whining child.

If you give your whining child attention by talking to her or giving her what she's whining for, you're teaching her that whining is the way to get what she wants.

Don't whine yourself.

Adult complaining may sound like whining to your child. If you're doing it, your preschool mimic will say to herself that it must be okay for her. If you're in a bad mood, don't get angry with your child because you're angry with the world. Simply tell your child that you're feeling out of sorts, but don't whine about it.

Don't get angry with your child.

Just because your child is having an off day, don't get angry yourself. She'll not only mistake your outbursts for attention, but your getting upset gives your child a feeling of power over you. She may continue to whine just to show you she's the boss.

Don't try to punish away crying and whining.

The old retort, "I'll give you something to really cry about," only creates conflict between you and your child and tells your child that it's never okay to cry, making her feel guilty for having disgruntled feelings. Allow crying and whining with restrictions, because crying may be the only way your child knows how to vent frustrations at the time, particularly if she's a pretalker.

Remember, this will not last forever.

Your child may be having a bad day or going through a period when nothing seems to please her, so she may spend more time whining and crying about life in general until she gets back in sync with her world. Tell yourself, "And this too shall pass," while you try to make life as least frustrating as possible for your child by praising any good behavior.

THE WHINING CHAIR

From the moment three-year-old Marsha Brenner woke up in the morning until she closed her eyes at night, she was a constant whirlwind of whining: "Mommy, I wanna eat! Mommy, what's on TV? Mommy, where are we going? Mommy, Mommy, pick me up, Mommy!"

Mrs. Brenner tried to ignore her daughter's noisemaking and gave in to her wants to get her to be quiet, but the sounds of her whining and whimpering started to grate on her nerves until one day she screamed, "Marsha! Stop that stupid whining. You sound horrible!"

Since her own yelling and screaming only increased Marsha's, Mrs. Brenner knew that she would have to use another method to stop her daughter's whining. She decided to try a version of Time Out, a technique she tried to use whenever her daughter misbehaved.

"This is the whining chair," she told her daughter the next morning, after she had begun her regular routine of whining. "I'm sorry that you are whining now. When you are done whining you can come out of the chair and we will play with your dolls," she stated, placing her daughter in the chair she had decided to use for this purpose. She then walked away, making sure she was not around to give her daughter any attention.

When Mrs. Brenner heard no more sounds from the direction of the whining chair, she returned to her daughter and praised her for stopping, "Oh, I love the way you're not whining. Now let's go play."

When Mrs. Brenner found her daughter spending time in the whining chair nearly ten times a day, she decided to take another step and teach Marsha how to stop herself from being put in the whining chair.

"When you ask me without whining, I will give you a drink," she explained that day, showing Marsha how to say, "Please, Mom, may I have a drink." Her daughter practiced the instructions when she wanted a drink, food, or toy that was previously whined for and not gotten.

Though Marsha's whining never completely ended (her mother realized that she sometimes still whined on her "off" days), Mrs. Brenner became much happier with her relationship with her daughter.

TALKING BACK

When backtalk—sarcasm, short retorts, and unpleasant side remarks—spews forth from your previously angelic preschooler's mouth, you become painfully aware of your child's ability to mimic words (good and bad) and control his world with them. Backtalk can only be learned (like all language) by exposure to it, so limit the opportunities your child has to hear unpleasant words. Monitor television, friends, and your own language, to eliminate backtalk from his vocabulary.

PREVENTING THE PROBLEM

Talk to your child as you want to be talked to.
Teach your child how to use language you want to hear. Say, "thank you," "please," and "I'm sorry." Also teach him that it's not always what he says but how he says it that is considered backtalk.

Decide what constitutes backtalk.
In order to react rationally to your child's increasingly diversified verbal behavior, you need to think about whether what your child says is backtalk or simply how he says words. Some distinctions might be these: sarcasm, name-calling, shouting answers, and defiant refusals are backtalk; simple refusals like "I don't want to" are whining; and questions like "Do I have to?" are expressions of opinion.

Monitor friends, media, and personal speech.
Keep tabs on what words slip through your lips and those of friends, peers, family, and television characters to limit the exposure your child has to backtalk.

Solving the Problem

Wear out the word.

Make your child tired of using the word you call backtalk so that in the heat of battle the word is rarely uttered. Tell him to practice saying the offending statement for one minute for each year of age to make the phrase lose its power. Say, "I'm sorry you said that word. I'll set the timer. You must say the word until the timer rings. When it rings, you can stop saying the word."

Ignore the backtalk.

Try to pay as little attention to inoffensive backtalk as you can. Pretending the event didn't even occur takes away any possible power the backtalker has over you and makes it no fun to talk back because it's not a fun game to play alone.

Compliment nice talk.

Let your child know what kind of talk you prefer him to use by pointing out when backtalk is not occurring. Say, "I like it when you don't shout back at me when I ask you a question. That was so nice of you." Tell him it's often how he says something that makes speech backtalk. Say, "I don't care" in an angry voice; then say it in a pleasant voice to illustrate your point.

Don't play "gotcha."

Since you know that backtalk is the way your child tries to get power over you, don't use backtalk yourself. He may find fun ways of entertaining himself by seeing how he can get you mad or get your attention by using backtalk, which you don't want to encourage.

Don't teach backtalk.

Shouting answers back to your child will only show him how to use backtalk. Although it's hard not to yell when you're being yelled at, try to teach your child how to be respectful by being respectful to him. Be polite to your child, as if he were a guest in your home.

Don't use severe punishment for backtalk.

Save your strongest punishment for really important, harmful behaviors that are dangerous to himself and others. Backtalk is, at worst, annoying. No evidence supports the belief that we make children respectful by punishing them for disrespect. Only fear is taught through punishment—not respect.

PAT'S BACKTALK

Whenever Mrs. Loren would ask her four-year-old son, Pat, to do anything like clean up his toys or put the peanut butter in the cabinet, Pat would shout, "No! I don't like you; I'm not going to!" Pat became so experienced at backtalk and verbal abuse that whenever he was asked *any* kind of question, he would angrily shout back his answer, as if he had forgotten how to answer someone politely.

"No child of mine is going to talk like that!" his father would shout back at his son, and *his* backtalk would get the family in an even greater uproar.

Once the Lorens realized that by being sarcastic and shouting back at their son they were modeling much of the behavior that Pat was picking up, they tried hard to react calmly to backtalk and to praise *any* pleasant response from him. "That's really great the way you answered so pleasantly," they said the first time they heard their son say, "Okay," when he was asked to put his toys in the toy box.

It was not hard for them to start controlling their anger, because both Mr. and Mrs. Loren noticed Pat yelling less and less and when they did hear sassy talk again, they usually pretended they hadn't heard the words.

But when Pat kept saying one word, "idiot," over and over, trying his hardest to get some attention, his parents decided to try to have Pat intentionally "wear out the word." "Say the word 'idiot' for four minutes," they instructed Pat. He said "idiot" as fast as he could for two minutes and then simply couldn't say it anymore, and much to the delight of his parents, it was the last time he said that word.

NAME-CALLING

Blossoming preschool linguists test out the power of calling people names to let the world know that they're the boss and can talk like it. Because you know your child's testing the word's strength as well as the reaction it gets, teach your child that name-calling will never cause the harm she thinks it might. React calmly to being called a name to burst the bubble of influence your child hopes name-calling will have. Help your child practice what you preach, as well, when she's the victim of name-calling; she'll see that this verbal game isn't much fun when played by one.

PREVENTING THE PROBLEM

Check pet names.

Avoid calling your child nicknames that you wouldn't want her to call someone else. There's a difference between saying, "You little devil" and "You little doll" to someone.

Teach substitutes for being a name-calling victim.

Suggest desirable ways for your child to react when she's the victim of a name-caller. Say, "When your friend calls you a bad name, tell her that you can't play with her when she calls you names."

Decide what's a bad name and what isn't.

Make sure you have educated your child about what names are not to be used before you expect her to know "legal" and "illegal" words.

SOLVING THE PROBLEM

Put your child in Time Out.

Remove your child from fun she's having for a specific length of time to say to her that when you do things that aren't approved, you lose your chances for playing. Say, "I'm sorry you called the name—time out." (See page 8 for more on Time Out.)

Wear out the name.

Wearing out the name helps make it less thrilling to say. Put your child in a chair and have her repeat the word without stopping (one minute for each year of age). If she refuses to do this (millions of independent preschoolers do), simply have her sit until she starts, no matter how long it takes.

Notice nice talk.

Praise your child when she's not calling names to show her what language you do and don't approve of her using.

Stick to your reactions.

Every time your child is the name-caller, use the same reaction to teach her that name-calling is never a game you want to play. Say, "I'm sorry you called a name. Now you'll have to go to Time Out," or "Now you must wear out the word," for example.

Don't show how to name-call.

Because being called names is so irritating, it's easy to shout back to your child the same ridiculous words she says to you, like, "You dummy! You should know better than to call names." This gives your preschooler permission to use the kinds of names you did. Channel your rage into an explanation of how and why you feel so upset, to teach your child when her words or actions make you happy or unhappy and how you'd like her to react when she feels like name-calling.

Don't use severe punishment for name-calling.

If you punish for name-calling, your child will only use the names when you are out of earshot. Using severe punishment for remedying misbehavior often teaches your child how to avoid getting caught. Punished behavior does not go away; it just goes out of sight.

"THAT'S NOT NICE!"

Max and Helen Glass were shocked when they first heard their precious four-and-a-half-year-old daughter, Sarah, call her friends, "dummy," "jerk," and, worst of all, "dog poo poo." They had never used those kinds of words around the house, so they couldn't understand where Sarah was picking them up, and they really didn't know what to do about it.

"Do not call people names, Sarah. That's not nice!" they would say every time their daughter used an offending word, but to no avail. In fact, Sarah soon began to even call her parents names, which caused them to spank her but didn't stop the name-calling.

Finally, Mrs. Glass tried another strategy: she began to oversee her daughter's playing more closely during the day and to pay attention to when she played well and when she didn't.

"How nicely you girls are getting along," she pointed out when Sarah and Maria, her cousin, were dressing their baby dolls.

But when Maria tried to take Sarah's doll for a ride in the blue car, Sarah yelled, "You dummy, Maria, you know that's *my* car."

Mrs. Glass immediately and calmly informed the girls that they would be separated now. "I'm sorry you called your cousin a 'dummy,' " she told her daughter. "Time out."

After four minutes (one minute for every year of age) in the Time-Out chair, Sarah soon learned that her mother meant what she said—playtime would be halted and Sarah would be ignored if she called anyone names. Sarah learned that it was better to get the approval of her parents and friends. Her name-calling grew more infrequent.

INTERRUPTING

Because a preschooler's most priceless possession is his parents' attention, he will try anything to get it back when the telephone, another person, or the doorbell takes it away. Limit the tricks your child tries to play to get your undivided attention by providing him with special playthings reserved for those times you chat with the competition. This will keep your child busy without you, while you're busy without him.

PREVENTING THE PROBLEM

Limit the length of conversations.

Knowing your child's ability to delay gratification is relatively limited, be a prudent parent by talking only for a short period of time while your child is near, unoccupied, and wanting your attention.

Practice play telephone.

Teach your child what you mean by not interrupting. Practice uninterruptive behavior with two play phones—one for each of you. Tell him, "This is how I talk on the phone, and this is how you play while I'm on the phone." Then let your child be the phone talker and you the onlooker. This defines interrupting for your child, as well as shows him what behaviors can replace interrupting.

Set up rules for telephone playtime.

Gather special toys and materials in a drawer near the phone (let over-two-year-olds choose themselves). While you're on the telephone, insist that your child play with those toys as you watch him and give facial and verbal attention by smiling as you tell your child how nicely he's playing. Finger paints, watercolors, Play-Doh, shaving cream, and magic markers for example, are toys that need supervision for preschoolers, so they should be within reach only when you are there to watch. Before you select toys for the drawer, think about how adept your child is at playing with them without parental supervision, to reduce your need to be interrupted just to control his play.

SOLVING THE PROBLEM

WHAT TO DO

Praise nice playing and not interrupting.

If your child is getting attention (smiles, praise, etc.) when he's being good and not interrupting, he won't need or want to barge in on your conversation to put in his two cents worth. Excuse yourself from whomever you are talking with and say to your child, "Thanks for playing so nicely with your doll. I'm so proud of you for having fun on your own."

Get your child involved with your life.

Try to include your child in your conversation when a friend visits you, for example, to lessen the chances that he will interrupt you to get recognized as being there.

WHAT NOT TO DO

Don't get angry and yell at your child for interrupting.

Don't encourage interrupting by showing your child how to do it.

Don't interrupt your child or others yourself.

Even if your child is a constant chatterbox, show him that you practice what you preach by not interrupting him when he's talking.

Use Grandma's Rule.

Let your child know that you will soon be all his again and that he can earn your attention by having fun while he waits for you. Use the timer to limit conversations; when it rings, let your child know he can now interact with you. Say, "When you have played with your toys for two minutes and the timer rings, I will be through talking on the phone and will play with you."

Reprimand and use Time Out.

Use a reprimand such as "Stop interrupting. I cannot talk to my friend while I'm being interrupted. Instead of interrupting, please play with your cars." If your child continues to interrupt, use Time Out to remove him from the possibility of immediately getting attention for interrupting. Say, "I'm sorry that you're continuing to interrupt—time out." (See page 8 for more on Time Out.)

"NOT NOW, JOANIE"

Whenever the phone rang, three-year-old Joanie Wilkens interrupted her mother's conversation with requests for drinks of apple juice, a toy in the "high place," or a question like, "Where are we going today?" Although she wanted to answer her daughter, Mrs. Wilkens tried to explain calmly at each interruption, "Sweetheart, Mommy is on the phone. Please don't interrupt."

But Joanie would only interrupt again, so one day Mrs. Wilkens started screaming, "Don't interrupt me! You are a bad girl!" giving her daughter a swift swat on the bottom to "shut her up." Not only did the swat *not* shut Joanie up, it angered her into crying and screaming so loudly that her mother could not continue her phone conversation.

The more her mother screamed, the more Joanie interrupted—a cause-and-effect relationship that Mrs. Wilkens finally understood and decided to reverse. She would now give her daughter attention for *not* interrupting instead of interrupting.

The next morning when her friend, Sally, called for her regular Monday morning chit-chat, Mrs. Wilkens informed her that she could not talk now because she was playing with the children, a rule she decided to try on herself to reduce the chances for her daughter to interrupt her on the phone.

As she explained this new policy to her friend, she noticed her daughter playing for a minute with her puzzle. "Thanks for not interrupting!" she complimented her daughter, giving her a big hug. Joanie began playing with the toys Mrs. Wilkens had gathered around the phone for this moment. The toys were especially fascinating to Joanie because they were called the 'telephone toys'—toys she was allowed to play with *only* when her mother was on the phone.

When she got off the phone, Mrs. Wilkens again praised Joanie, "Thanks for not interrupting me while I told Sally about our dinner tonight," she explained. "She wanted a recipe for meat loaf," she said. "These markers are here for you to play with, if you want, while I talk on the phone."

The next time the phone rang, a smile of anticipation instead of a frown of mischief crossed Joanie's and her mother's face. "Joanie, the phone is ringing. Let's play with the telephone toys," Mrs. Wilkens suggested. Joanie ran to get the markers, and an occasional "nice playing" helped her keep busy under her mother's watchful eye during the telephone conversation.

AGGRESSIVE BEHAVIOR

Like bulls in china closets, many energetic little dynamos under six years old hurl toys or themselves at the nearest targets when frustrated, angry, or just in rambunctious spirits. Why? Because reasoning or compromising is not one of their problem-solving techniques and throwing books or toys doesn't seem any more wrong than tossing balls. Tame your child by educating her about properly getting along with others. Briefly show and tell (even your one-year-old) what may be acceptably done to other people and toys (Illegal: hitting, biting, throwing, teasing; Legal: kissing, hugging, talking), and why these actions are good or bad. Strictly and consistently enforce the rules to help guide your child on the path of appropriate behavior, not destruction to herself and others.

Note: If your child's aggressive behavior is a regular feature of her daily "getting along" play and is disruptive to friends, family, and yourself, seek professional help to find out what may lie underneath your child's angry and frustrated play.

PREVENTING THE PROBLEM

Supervise play closely.
To prevent your child from learning aggressive behavior from her peers, monitor how she and her friends are caring for their toys. Don't let aggressive behavior cause injury or damage; do unto your child's friends' misbehavior as you would do unto your own child's.

Don't teach aggressive behavior.
Do to your things what you want your children to do to theirs. For

example, hitting and throwing things when you're angry shows your
child how to be aggressive when she's mad.

Point out biting and hitting when you see someone else doing it.
At a neutral time, explain how it's making the other person feel to be
bitten or hit—to let your child see just how unpleasant aggressive
behavior is for both sides.

SOLVING THE PROBLEM

WHAT TO DO

Tell your child what to do besides hit.
When aggressive behavior starts, give your child a list of things to do
besides hit when she's feeling upset. Tell your child that she can do
things like ask for help or say, "I'm not playing anymore," and simply
leave the group of kids for a minute. Have her practice saying those lines
five times after you to familiarize her with the words and how to use
them.

Compliment getting along.
Point out what getting along is and what it isn't by telling your child how
much you like how she shares, takes turns, or asks for help. Simply say,
"Good sharing with your friends, honey," always being specific about
what you're praising. The more praise, the friendlier the group or
individual behavior.

Use reprimands.
Reprimand your child to help her understand that you're not going to
stop a behavior for no reason at all—and you respect her ability to
understand why you interrupted it. The three parts to a reprimand
include giving a command to stop ("Stop hitting!"), giving an alternative
to hitting ("When you're angry, just leave the group."), and providing a
reason for stopping ("Hitting hurts!"). If your child continues being
aggressive, repeat the reprimand, adding Time Out to give more power to
the situation.

Forget the incident when it's over.
Reminding your child about past aggression doesn't teach her not to be
aggressive; it just reminds her of how she could be again.

WHAT NOT TO DO

Don't use aggression to stop aggression.
Your hitting only gives your child permission to hit in certain
circumstances.

Don't let off steam when your child is.
Your getting angry when your child hits only suggests to your child that
she can use aggression to get power over you.

MIKE THE BITER

At twenty-two months of age, Mike Meyer had become known as the
neighborhood biter, having had a lot of practice on two older brothers
who teased him mercilessly. Mrs. Meyer would threaten her youngest
child in order to stop his aggressiveness: "If you don't stop biting people,
Mikey, I'm going to spank you," but she knew that she never intended to
fulfill her threat.

Mike's three- and five-year-old brothers' teasing didn't seem to bother
their mother; in fact, their whole family joked about everything and she
considered their making fun of Mikey all in the spirit of not taking yourself too seriously. Her husband didn't agree. "Think how all that teasing
about being a baby brother must make Mike feel," he said one day.

Though she didn't want to admit it, Mrs. Meyer had never thought about
this problem from Mike's point of view—that *he* teased by biting because
he couldn't match his brothers' verbal attacks. She decided to discipline
all three boys for any kind of attack—biting, hitting, teasing, and throwing things would not be allowed. That was the only way, she decided, to
teach the older boys to be models of good behavior and to teach Mike to
make a choice about what kind of playing brought him attention and
praise.

The next day, Mike began to bite his brothers as usual when they called
him a "little Oscar the Grouch." Mrs. Meyer reprimanded Mike first:
"Stop biting. We bite apples, not people. Biting hurts people," she said
calmly but firmly. She also reprimanded Mike's brothers: "Stop teasing.
We do not tease people, because it hurts their feelings," she explained.

When the reprimands didn't stop the boys' verbal and physical attacks,
Mrs. Meyer continued, "I'm sorry that you are biting and teasing each
other. Time Out." The three of them were then directed to separate
chairs and told when they could play again.

As Mrs. Meyer became consistent in her discipline and praised any getting-along that the boys did within the home, all the Meyer boys learned

what to expect from fighting and from being friendly—which brought rewards and made life better than being isolated in a chair throughout the day. Mike began to bite less since he didn't have to compete with his brothers' teasing.

GETTING INTO THINGS

Just getting into first gear in their first year, one-year-olds feel the joy of exploration from their toes to their teeth. If given no restraints, everything and everyone is within their reach, by knees or soles. Your one-year-old doesn't automatically know what are no's and yes's, though by two and older he's able to make the distinction once you've set him straight. While restricting the adventures of your little wanderers, keep in mind the balance you're trying to strike in all the preschool years (and older) between letting normal, healthy curiosity be expressed and teaching what is and isn't appropriate for your child to do in and out of your home.

PREVENTING THE PROBLEM

Childproof your house.

Keeping doors closed and areas fenced off and supervising young travelers will limit the number of times you say no in a day and make life less dangerous for you and your child. Children under three years old can't understand why they may not go where they want, particularly when they're trying so hard to establish their independence and make their mark on the world. (See Appendix 1, page 131, for more on childproofing.)

Decide what may and may not be touched.

Decide what is legal and let your child in on the distinction when he is as young as possible. Say, "You may play in here or there," for example, "but not in Daddy's office."

Put away no-no's that must not break.

A one-, two-, or three-year-old will not understand the difference between a precious vase that's been left within his reach and the one-dollar variety. Play it safe by removing those items that must not be broken, until little minds and hands won't try to grab for everything despite being instructed not to.

Teach how your child can go into off-limits areas.

Explain to your child the legal ways to go into off-limits areas, because never being allowed to go into a room or across the street, for example, makes him want to do it more. Say, for instance, "You can go into Mommy's office, but only with Mommy or another adult."

SOLVING THE PROBLEM

WHAT TO DO

Use reprimands.

Consistently reprimand your child for the same offense to teach him you mean what you say. Say, "Stop going into that room! I'm sorry you were playing in here. You know this is off-limits. I'd like you to ask Mommy to come with you if you want to go into this room."

Put your child in Time Out.

If your child climbs on the kitchen table repeatedly (and if that's a no-no), reprimand him again and say "time out," putting him in Time Out to strengthen the reminder. (See page 8 for more on Time Out.)

Keep track of when your child follows the rules.

Tell your child how proud you are of him for remembering not to touch certain things. Giving him that compliment will reward his behavior with attention and promote his wanting to do the right thing again. Say, "How nice of you to play in here where you are supposed to," or "Thanks for not climbing on the coffee table."

Teach your child to touch with his eyes, not his hands.

Tell your child that he may look at a piece of jewelry, or vase, or picture, for example, with his eyes, but not with his hands. This allows him the freedom to explore the desirable item in a limited, controlled way.

WHAT NOT TO DO

Don't make no-no's more inviting.

If you become angry when your child breaks a rule, he'll see that he can get your attention from misbehavior and be encouraged to get into trouble more often.

Don't use severe punishment.

Reprimands and Time Out are okay, however, because they won't damage your child's self-esteem or confuse him into thinking that all he has to do is break something to get you to pay attention to him.

"Do Not Touch!"

"Curiosity killed the cat" was the line that Mrs. Stein remembered her mother saying to her when she'd climb up on off-limits counters as a toddler. Now she found her fifteen-month-old son, Sam, exploring forbidden lamps and plants; she knew he wasn't being intentionally bad—just behaving like a normal child. But Mrs. Stein didn't think her reactions to his curiosity seemed normal or showed much self-discipline.

"No! Do not touch!" she would shout, slapping her son's hands or spanking him whenever he got into things he knew were no-no's.

Mrs. Stein realized that Sam had committed all the crimes by prowling around behind her back, learning to avoid all the costs for getting caught at being unlawfully curious. So she decided to lock up as many things as possible, to put breakables out of reach, and to try to be with him as much as possible.

"Touch with your eyes, not your hands," she said to him on one particularly active morning when he had started taking everything out of her jewelry box, one item she had forgotten to put on the top shelf. She moved the box and guided her son back to the kitchen where they both had a good time taking all of the pots and pans out of the cabinet. They also played with the key and lock box and several other toys that provided stimulation for his imagination and curiosity—toys that were appropriate for his age and appropriate for him to take apart and try to destroy.

Once Sam had things within his reach that he could legally play with, the Steins began having a safer household. Though Mrs. Stein still knew she would have to monitor her son's curiosity, she let him have more freedom than before since her house was more childproof.

She knew that Sam was learning the "rules" of the roost when he took hold of a sack of flour he was told not to play with and said, "No! Mommy's, do not touch." To reward his good behavior, his mother handed him a sealed box of rice, which he loved to shake like a rattle.

DESTROYING PROPERTY

The line between destructive and creative play is not drawn for preschoolers until parents etch it in stone for them. So, before your child reaches her first birthday, draw the line by telling (and showing) her what she can and can't paint, tear up, or take apart, for example, to prevent your budding artist from doing unintentional damage to her and others' property. Consistently teach your child to have pride in and care for her and others' things while you let her creative juices flow in appropriate times and places—on drawing paper, not wallpaper, or with a take-apart play phone, not your real telephone.

PREVENTING THE PROBLEM

Provide toys that are strong enough to be investigated but not destroyed.
It's natural for preschoolers to try to take apart and put together toys that lend themselves to this kind of activity, as well as ones that won't. Fill your child's play area with toys that do things (stacking toys, push-button games) instead of those that just sit there (like the piano that you can't play) in order to stimulate the kind of creative play you want to encourage.

Give her things to wear and tear.
Provide plenty of old clothes and paper for papier-mâché, dress-up, painting, or other activities so your preschooler won't substitute new and precious materials for her own innocent projects.

Share specific rules about caring for and playing with toys.
Since children don't innately know the value of things or how to play with everything, teach them about newspapers and novels, for example. Say, "Your coloring book is the only thing you can color on with your

crayons. Nothing else is for crayons." "Books are not for tearing. If you want to tear, ask me and I will give you something." Or, "This wax apple does not come apart and cannot be eaten like a real one. If you'd like an apple to eat, I'll give you one."

Supervise your child's play.

Keep an intermittent eye on your child while she's playing because you can't expect her to care for things the way you would.

Be consistent about what's playing and what's destroying.

Don't confuse your child and make her test the legal waters over and over again by letting her destroy something she shouldn't. She won't know what to expect and won't understand when you destroy her fun by punishing her for a no-no that was formerly a yes-yes.

Remind her about caring.

Increase your chances for keeping destruction to a minimum by letting your child know when she is taking wonderful care of her toys. This reminds her of the rule, helps her feel good about herself, and makes her proud of her possessions.

SOLVING THE PROBLEM

WHAT TO DO

Overcorrect the mess.

If your child is over two years old, teach her to take care of her things by having her help clean up the messes she makes. If, for example, your child writes on the wall, she must clean not only the writing, but all the walls in the room. This overcorrection of the problem gives your child a sense of ownership and caring as well as teaches her how to clean walls!

Use reprimands.

If your child is under two, briefly give her a reprimand (tell her what she did, why it was wrong, and what she should have done) to help her understand why she's been taken away from her fun.

Put your child in Time Out.

If you've given your child a reprimand and your child destroys property again, repeat the reprimand and put her in Time Out. (See page 8 for more on this.)

WHAT NOT TO DO

Don't expect too much.

If your child breaks something, don't throw a tantrum yourself. Your anger communicates the idea that you care more for your things than you do your child. Make sure your degree of disappointment over something being destroyed isn't out of proportion to what happened.

Don't use severe punishment.

If no danger was incurred or could have been by your child's activities, concentrate on teaching your child how to care for things correctly instead of focusing on the wrongdoing.

TIM THE TERROR

Walt and Becky Brady knew they had a "destructive" three-year-old child long before the preschool teacher called them in for a conference about Tim. They could have bent Tim's teacher's ears with tales of his creations with purple crayon on the yellow daisy dining room wallpaper or the mosaics he made out of the pages of their hardcover books.

"When are you going to stop all this destruction, Tim?" Mr. Brady screamed, as he spanked his son and sent him to his room. The babysitter had just told him that Tim had drawn on the tile floor with crayon while his parents were at their conference. For the thousandth time, they had to repeat the punishment an hour later when Mr. Brady found that Tim had torn up three of his picture books while he was in his room.

They decided that they would have to make their misbehaving son pay the price for his destructive behavior. The next time they found Tim tearing a book's page, they didn't threaten or spank him. "Now you will have to fix this book, Tim," they stated, taking Tim by the hand to where the tape was kept and helping him tear off the appropriate amount and patch up the book.

Not only did Tim have to fix *that* book, but for three or four days after that, Tim washed the walls, scraped crayon off tiles, and taped back cards that were slightly damaged by a rip here or there—activities he never repeated once he paid for his misbehavior.

Each time something was damaged, Mr. and Mrs. Brady explained what could be torn and what could not be torn. After several days of learning that he had to be just as responsible for his family's possessions as his parents were, Tim began to earn that importance placed upon him. He beamed with pride when his parents praised him for caring for his books, records, and stuffed animals in a responsible way, and he dropped his head in shame when he slipped back into his old destructive habits.

As Tim's behavior became less destructive, his parents still didn't expect him to care for his toys as they did their adult toys, but they were careful to model neat behavior so that Tim could see how they practiced what they preached about respecting property.

TAKING THINGS

Since everything in the world belongs to a preschooler until someone tells him differently, it's never too early to teach him not to take things from others unless you approve it. Parents are their children's consciences until the time they develop them. So every time your child takes things that aren't his, enforce the consequences to keep him legal, now and after he's out from under your wing.

PREVENTING THE PROBLEM

Make rules.

Encourage your child to inform you when he wants things by teaching him how to ask for them. Decide what may and may not be taken from public places or others' homes, and let your child know that game plan. A basic rule might be "You must always ask me if you can have something before you pick it up."

SOLVING THE PROBLEM

WHAT TO DO

Explain how to get things without stealing.

Your child may not understand why he cannot take things he sees when he wants to, so you must make him aware of correct and incorrect behavior. Say, "You may ask me for a piece of gum; if I say yes, you may pick up the package and hold it until we pay for it."

Be consistent.

Don't let your child take something from the grocery store shelf one day but not the next time you go shopping. This will only confuse him when he's trying to decide for himself what can and cannot be his.

Show what you mean by stealing.

Educate your child about the difference between borrowing and stealing and the results of each, to make sure he knows what you mean when you say, "You must not steal."

Let your child pay for stealing.

To help him realize the cost of stealing, have your child work off the theft by doing odd jobs around the house or giving up one of his prized possessions. Say, for example, "I'm sorry that you took something that didn't belong to you. Because you did that, you must give up something that belongs to you." The possession he gives up could be used several months later as a reward for good behavior.

Make children return stolen objects.

Teach your child that he cannot keep things that aren't his or are borrowed without permission. Enforce the rule that he returns it himself (with you, if necessary).

Enforce Time Out.

When your child takes something that doesn't belong to him, let him know that he must be isolated from people and activities because he broke the rule. Say, "I'm sorry that you took something that wasn't yours. Time out." (See page 8 for more on Time Out.)

WHAT NOT TO DO

Don't be a historian.

Don't remind your child about a stealing incident. Bringing up the past will only reteach him what to do wrong, not right.

Don't label your child.

Don't call your child a thief, for example, because he will begin to behave according to how he's labeled.

Don't ask your child whether he stole something.

Asking only encourages lying. "I know I'll be punished. Why not lie to avoid the pain?" he says to himself.

Don't hesitate to search your child.

If you suspect your child has stolen something, verify it yourself by searching him. Use consequences if you find he did steal. Say, "I'm sorry you took something that didn't belong to you," and use "what to do" procedures.

THE SHORT SHOPLIFTER

Sandy and Doug Berkley had never broken the law and gone to jail, and they didn't want their four-year-old son, Scott, to get locked behind bars for doing so, either. But if he kept picking up gum, candy, toys, and any other object that caught his fancy when he and his parents were shopping, they wondered (half seriously) if he'd have a future outside of prison.

"Don't you know that stealing is wrong?" Mrs. Berkley would scream at her son when she'd catch him red-handed, slapping his hand and telling him he was a bad boy. She became afraid to do her errands with her son, dreading the embarrassment she felt for the physical punishment she thought she had to dish out.

But Scott was totally oblivious to the reasons why stealing was forbidden. The Berkleys finally decided that he could not possibly understand that it was not fun to take what didn't belong to him. So they began to explain the situation in terms their son could understand.

"Scott, you cannot take things that you do not pay for," Mr. Berkley began. "You may ask me for a pack of gum, and if I say yes, you may pick up the package and hold it until we pay for it. Let's practice."

Scott was delighted to oblige because now when he asked for gum, as the rule stated, his mother and father complimented him for following the rules and paid for the gum.

When Scott tried to get by with taking a candy bar without first asking his mother to pay for it, Mrs. Berkley enforced her second rule by making him "pay" for the wrongdoing. "Because you took this candy bar," she told her son as they walked back into the store, "you will have to give up the toy candy bar that is in your grocery store at home."

Despite the protests from her son, she *did* take away the toy he loved. "To earn the toy back," his mother explained, "you will have to follow the rules by asking first and not taking what is not paid for," his mother explained when they got home.

After several weeks of her praising Scott for following the rules, the toy candy bar was again made part of his grocery store, and Mr. and Mrs. Berkley felt more secure about their frisky little son's future.

POSSESSIVENESS

The word "mine" is the password preschoolers use to remind each other (and adults) that they own their world and are important enough to have territorial rights whenever and however they want. Despite the wars that this four-letter word incites in all households with under-five-year-olds, possessiveness will be alive and well until children are developmentally ready to let it die (between three and four years old). Help more peacetime prevail before and after your preschooler can enter a settlement about what is hers and what isn't by consistently teaching your child the give-and-take rules of the world. Enforce these sharing rules at your house, but be patient. Don't expect them to be righteously followed until you see your child sharing without your intervention—the glorious sign that she's ready to broaden her boundaries.

PREVENTING THE PROBLEM

Make sure some toys strictly belong to your child.

Before preschoolers can let go of the word "mine" and the things they attach to it, they must be given the chance to possess things. For example, put away favorite toys or blankets so they will not have to be shared when visitors play at your house. This will keep some territory your child's very own.

Point out how you and your friends share.

Show your child that she isn't the only one in the world expected to share her things. Give examples at neutral (nonsharing) times of how you and your friends share books (say, "Mary borrowed my cookbook today" or "Charlie borrowed my lawnmower.")

Point out what sharing means and how much you like it.

Tell your child how nicely she's sharing whenever she allows another person to look at or play with her toy to make sharing as attractive as possible. Say, "I like the way you're sharing by letting your friend have that toy for a minute," for example.

Put labels on some toys (for twins or children close in age).

Make sure you don't confuse your child's teddy bear with her sister's or brother's, for example, if they are the same. Label each one with a name or piece of thread to help your child feel confident that everything that's hers is not also her brother's or sister's.

Set up sharing rules.

Before friends come to play, let your child know what's expected of her at group sharing times. For example, teach her this rule: If you put a toy down, anyone may play with it. If you have it in your hands, you may keep it.

Understand that your child may share better at a friend's house.

Because it's not your child's territory, she may play a more passive role when at someone else's house and take a more possessive, aggressive role at hers.

Remember that sharing is a developmental task.

Learning to share is an accomplishment that cannot be rushed. Usually at three to four years of age, your child will begin to share things on her own without being reminded.

SOLVING THE PROBLEM

WHAT TO DO

Supervise one- and two-year-olds' play.

Because children younger than three years old cannot be expected to share, stay close by while they're playing to help resolve sharing conflicts they are too young to handle without help.

Set the timer.

When two children are calling a toy "mine," show how the give-and-take of sharing works. Tell one child that you will be setting the timer and when the timer rings, the other child can have the toy. Keep doing the timer routine until they have grown tired of the toy (usually two rings later).

Put toys in Time Out.

If a toy is the root of the problem because one child will not share, put the sought-after toy in Time Out to put it out of the children's reach. If the toy is not with the children, it cannot cause any trouble. Say, "This toy is causing trouble; it must go into Time Out." If the children keep fighting over the toy after it has been brought out, keep removing the toy to make the point that not sharing a toy means that no one plays with that toy. (See page 8 for more on Time Out.)

WHAT NOT TO DO

Don't get upset.

Remember that your child will learn the rule about sharing when she can, not by force or demanding from you. When you see your child sharing— you'll know she's ready!

Don't punish for occasionally not sharing.

Remove the offending toy rather than punish your child if she occasionally cannot share something. This puts the blame on the toy, not the child.

LEARNING TO SHARE

Three-year-old Mark Gold knew what the word "sharing" meant—it meant that he could not sit and hold as many toys as he wanted to whenever his friend Jim came over to play with him.

"You *must* share!" Mark's mother told her son after another day of Mark clutching as many toys as possible and saying "mine" wherever his mother said, "Now, Mark, let's share."

"I'm going to give all your toys to poor children who will appreciate them," Mrs. Gold screamed one day, threatening and finally spanking Mark into tearfully giving up his toys.

That night after their son was tucked in bed, Mrs. Gold told her husband, "Mark just doesn't know *how* to share," a statement that Mr. Gold thought shed new light on the problem. Both he and his wife decided that they needed to *teach* Mark specifically what sharing meant.

The next time Mark's mother knew he was soon to be in the company of his two cousins, she took him aside for a talk. "Mark, here's the sharing rule. Anyone can play with anything in this house as long as another person is not holding it. If you or Mike or Mary are holding a toy, for example, no one can take it away. Each of you may only play with one toy at a time." Mark and his mother then decided what toy Mark could just not bear to have out of his clutches and put it away so it wouldn't be the cause of dissension during his cousins' visit.

The next few hours were tense for Mrs. Gold, but Mark seemed to be more relaxed. He began by holding only one toy and letting his cousins have their pick of the lot in the toy box. "I'm so proud of you for sharing," his watchful mother praised him as she oversaw the operation.

When she ventured off to fix lunch, the familiar "mine" cry brought her back to the playroom. The new "burp-itself" doll was being pulled limb from limb by Mary and Mark. "This toy is causing trouble," Mrs. Gold stated matter-of-factly; "it must go to Time Out." All the children stared in disbelief as they watched poor Betsy sitting in the Time-Out chair, looking as lonely as a misbehaved pooch. After two minutes Mrs. Gold returned the toy to the children, who had long since forgotten about it and were busy playing with blocks.

As the weeks went by, all the children played side by side with fewer Time Outs needed to restore peace, particularly since Mark was more open to letting "his" toys be "their" toys during the play period.

FIGHTING CLEANUP ROUTINES

From a no-more-tears formula shampoo to disposable diapers, products abound to make bathing, diapering, and shampooing as palatable as possible to preschoolers and their parents. It's expected and even predicted (as these manufacturers know) that preschoolers will find cleaning routines distasteful, so don't feel alone as you persevere with rinsing and soaking. Try to make the cleaning tasks less tedious by diverting your child's attention (sing songs, tell stories) and praising any cooperation (even handing you the soap).

Note: Make the distinction between what products irritate your child physically (does it burn eyes?) and mentally (are all soaps undesirable?) by seeing whether his protests are telling you more than just that he doesn't like the cleaning event. Switch from products that irritate the skin to those professionally recommended, if necessary.

PREVENTING THE PROBLEM

Compromise on cleanup time and place.

Try to make compromises with your child about issues like where you diaper him (on the couch, standing up) or when you wash his hair. Be flexible so your child will not miss a favorite walk just to get his hair washed or miss an episode of a parent-approved television program just to have his diaper changed.

Involve your child in the process.

Help your child play a part in the routine of cleaning himself or diapering. Ask him to bring you things he can carry, according to his age, skill level, and ability to follow directions. Let him pick a favorite toy or towel, for example, as a bath companion to give him a feeling of having some control in the cleaning routine.

Prepare your child for the coming event.

Give your child some warning before a bath, for example, to make the change from playing to bathing less abrupt. Say, "When the timer rings, it will be time for the tub," or "In a few minutes, we will change diapers," or "When we finish this book, it will be time for your bath."

Gather materials before starting.

If your child is too young to help you prepare, make sure you have your ammunition at hand before going to the cleanup "war." This gets the process on the way without unnecessary delay.

Develop a positive attitude.

Your child will pick up on the dread in your voice if you announce bathtime like it's a sentence to jail, and he will decide it's really as horrible as he thought if you are worried about it, too. Since your attitude is contagious, make it one you want imitated.

SOLVING THE PROBLEM

WHAT TO DO

Remain calm and ignore the noise.

A calm mood in dealing with your upset child will be contagious. If you don't pay attention to the noise, your child will learn that lots of noise has no power over you, which is what he wants when he's resisting your cleaning him up. Say to yourself, "I know my child needs to be diapered. If I don't give his noise any attention, I'll get this done faster and more effectively."

Have fun in the process.

Talk and play with your child while he's struggling by saying nursery rhymes and singing to distract his attention. Say, "Let's sing 'Old MacDonald,' " or "I'll bet you can't catch this boat and make it dive into the water." Simply make it a monologue if your child's too young to participate verbally.

Encourage his help and shower your child with praise.

Ask your child to wash his own tummy, rub on the soap, or open the diaper (if time permits) to give him a feeling of controlling and participating in his personal hygiene. Even the slightest sign of cooperation is a signal for praise. Lather on the words of encouragement—the more your child gets attention for acting like you'd prefer, the more he'll repeat the action to get your strokes. Say, "I really

Fighting Cleanup Routines

like how you put that shampoo on your hair," or "That's great the way you're sitting up in the tub," or "Thanks for lying down so nicely while I diaper you."

Enforce Grandma's Rule.

Let your child know that when he's done something you want him to do (take a bath), he can do what he'd like (read a story). Say, "When your bath is over, then we will have a story," or "When we're finished, then you can play."

Persist in the task at hand.

Despite the kicking, screaming, and yelling about becoming neat and clean, remember that you're going to finish the process. The more your child sees that yelling isn't going to prevent you from washing away the dirt, the more he'll understand that you can get the job done faster if he takes the path of least resistance.

Compliment the sweet and soft.

Tell your child how delightful he looks and smells; ask him to go look in the mirror to remind him about why he needs to have a bath or diaper changed. Your preschooler's learning to take pride in himself will help him to incorporate the desire to keep clean into his own priorities as well as yours.

WHAT NOT TO DO

Don't demand cooperation.

Just because you demand that your child gets diapered, for instance, doesn't mean he's going to lie still while you do it. Acting rough and tough only teaches him how to do it, too.

Don't make cleanup painful.

Try to provide towels with which your child can wipe his eyes, bathwater at a temperature that feels just right, or a wrap-up robe for him to step into, for example, to make cleanup as comfortable as possible.

Don't avoid cleanup.

Just because your child resists, don't back down on the cause of cleanliness. Resistance to cleanup can be overcome by persistence.

"OCEANS OF FUN"

Carol and Phil Porter bathed and shampooed their two-year-old daughter, Pam, just as they thought most of the parents they knew did. But they feared that something was wrong with Pam to make her scream and fight her way through these normal cleanup processes; none of the Porters' friends ever complained about this problem, and they had never experienced it with their other daughter, Elizabeth, now four years old.

Knowing they couldn't simply forego cleaning up their daughter, Mr. and Mrs. Porter devised ways to make cleanup more appetizing to their daughter after her pediatrician had assured them that the soaps, water, and towels they used were not harmful or irritating. "Doesn't she like *anything* about cleaning up?" he had asked.

The only water-related activity the Porters knew their daughter loved was swimming in the Pacific Ocean on their vacation each summer, so they decided to call the bathtub "Oceans of Fun," even though Mr. Porter thought stricter discipline was needed.

So the following evening the Porters tried it. They first set a timer to ring when it was time to get in the "ocean." In California, they had always set a timer to signal the time to go to the real ocean because Pam was always begging to get in the water there. They hoped the discipline would prove positive at home in Minneapolis, too. "When the timer rings, it will be time for you to play the new game," Mrs. Porter said to Pam the first night. "Let's finish this book while we're waiting."

When the timer rang to announce bathtime, both Pam and her mother gathered towels and soap, as Pam excitedly asked dozens of questions about this new game and where the ocean was.

Pam smiled with delight as her mom led her to the bathroom where she found the bluest ocean she'd ever seen (the result of blue bubblebath) and jaunty boats cruising around a toy ship holding a container of soap, toys Mrs. Porter had bought to add to the experience.

Pam jumped in without a push, shove, or even an invitation and began playing with the ocean toys; her mother started to sing a song about a tugboat, and Pam was given a palmful of shampoo to "do her own hair" for the first time.

The experience continued without yelling or screaming and probably just a little too much splashing. But the two enjoyed the cleanup so much that Mrs. Porter began bathing Pam in the "ocean" at least once a day to give her more opportunities to learn how to splash less, wash herself more carefully, and enjoy the experience instead of dread it.

MESSINESS

Little people make big messes, and unfortunately for orderly parents, small children are almost always oblivious to their self-made clutter. Knowing that your child is not messy, but simply unaware of the need to clean up after herself, teach her (the younger the better) that messes don't disappear magically—the mess maker (and helpers) clean them up. Share this fact of life with your child, but don't expect perfection in her following the rule. Encourage rather than demand neatness by praising the slightest attempt your child makes at playing the cleanup game.

PREVENTING THE PROBLEM

Clean up as you go along.
For example, show your child how to put away her toys immediately after she's done playing to limit clutter as she bounces from plaything to plaything. Help your child pick up the picking-up habit early in life to encourage her to be a neater child and, later, a more organized adult.

Show her how to clean up her mess.
Provide appropriately sized boxes and cans, for instance, in which your child can physically put away her toys, clay, etc. Show her how the things fit inside the container and where the container goes when filled, to eliminate the possibility that she just doesn't know what you mean when you ask her to put something away or clean something up.

Be as specific as you can.
Instead of asking your child to clean up her room, tell her exactly what you'd like cleaned up. Say, for instance, "Let's put the pegs in the bucket and the blocks in the box," to make it as simple as possible for your child to follow your directions.

Provide adequate cleanup supplies.

Don't expect your child to know what to use to clean up her mess all by herself. Give her the right cloth to wash the table off, for example, praising all the efforts she puts into the cleaning after you've given her the tools of the trade.

Confine activities to a safe place.

Make sure you let your child perform messy play (painting, clay) in the least vulnerable places. Don't expect her to know not to destroy the living room carpet when you've let her fingerpaint in there, for example.

SOLVING THE PROBLEM

What to do

Use Grandma's Rule.

If your child refuses to clean up a mess she's made, make her fun dependent on doing the job you request. Say, for example, "Yes, I know that you don't want to pick up blocks. But when you have picked them up, you may go outside to play." Remember that your child (one year and older) can help in the cleanup process in even a small way, and she needs to try her best at whatever level she can, slowly building up to more difficult tasks.

Assist in cleanup jobs.

Sometimes the cleanup job is too big for a child's muscles or hands. Join in the work to encourage sharing and cooperation, two lessons you want your child to learn at the preschool level. Seeing Mom or Dad clean up, for example, makes cleaning up that much more of an inviting and reasonable activity.

Play Beat-the-Clock.

When made into a game of beating the timer, picking up toys changes from being an arduous task to a fun game. Join in the fun by saying, for example, "When you've picked up the toys before the timer rings, you can take out another toy." When your child is successful at beating the clock, praise her accomplishment and follow through on your promise.

Praise any cleaning effort.

Encourage your child to clean up after herself by using a powerful motivator—praise! Comment about the great job she's doing while she's putting her crayons away by saying, "I really am glad that you put that red crayon in the basket. Thanks for helping to clean up your room."

Don't expect perfection.

Your child has had only a few thousand days to practice cleaning up after herself, so don't expect her job to be perfect. Just the fact that she tries means she's learning how to do the chore; she will improve with practice and age.

Don't punish messiness.

Your child cannot yet understand the value of neatness and doesn't have the physical maturity to stay tidy. "My parents leave their toys lying about, so why can't I?" your child may say to herself when she sees ashtrays, newspapers, or pens on the coffee table.

Don't expect children to prepare themselves for messes.

Your child does not know the value of nice clothing. Provide old ones to put on backwards, for example, instead of expecting her to keep her expensive ones tidy while she paints.

MULTIPLE MESSES

John and Bev Wareman were getting used to everything but the mess of toys their almost-five-year-old twins, Margaret and Mandy, made almost daily.

"Good chidren always put their toys away," Mrs. Wareman told them, trying to convince the girls not to leave their toys in the living room when they were done playing.

When that didn't work, however, she began to spank her daughters and put them in their rooms when they didn't clean up their chaos, a punishment that seemed only to punish her because of the additional mess the girls created when they were in isolation.

Mrs. Wareman saw a way to resolve this dilemma when she realized how much the children liked to play outside on their new swing set. She decided to turn that activity into a privilege that had to be earned and was not freely awarded without a cost. One day when the girls wanted to go outside instead of putting back the pegs and the kitchen set they had been playing with, she said, "Here's the new rule, girls. I know you want to go outside, but when you have picked up your kitchen set, Margaret, and your pegs, Mandy, you can do that. I will help."

The two girls looked at each other. They didn't want to do any picking up, but they had never heard it put like that before. Mrs. Wareman began helping put the pegs in the jar to make sure that Mandy knew just what "clean up the pegs" meant. She then opened up the bag so Margaret could deposit the kitchen utensils in their proper home, leaving no doubt about what cleaning up the kitchen set meant.

As the girls and their mother did the chores together, Mrs. Wareman left no doubt, too, about how happy she was with their efforts. "Thanks for cleaning up. You're doing a great job filling that jar with the pegs. I sure like the way that kitchen fits into that tiny bag," she commented, hugging each girl with genuine pride in her accomplishment. Soon both children spilled out the door, leaving mother to fix lunch instead of cleaning up after them.

For many weeks, the girls needed to be offered a reward for cleaning up a mess, but they did finally learn that putting away one toy before taking out another made the cleanup process quicker and brought all those compliments from Mom.

SIBLING RIVALRY

Tattling on brothers and sisters and hating a new sibling from the first day he invades the family—these are just two examples of how sibling rivalry wreaks havoc on family relationships. Because preschoolers are constantly flapping their wings of independence and importance, they often fight with their siblings for the space, time, and place of being number one in their most important world—their family. Though sibling rivalry is a fact of life in the most amiable of family relationships because of the competitive nature of human beings, its frequency can be decreased by encouraging each of your preschoolers to feel he's special—one of a kind. To keep sibling rivalry to a manageable minimum, show that getting along reaps other benefits like attention and privileges.

Note: To decrease the sibling rivalry centered around a new baby, make sure you play with your older child when the new baby is awake as well as asleep. This will prevent your first child from equating your giving him attention with the baby's being out of sight. Spending time together makes older children think, "I get Mom's attention when the baby's here as well as gone. That baby's not so bad after all!"

PREVENTING THE PROBLEM

Prepare your child before a new baby invades his world.
Discuss with your first child (if he's over one year old) how he will be included in the life of the new baby. Tell him what the family's daily life will consist of when the baby arrives. This helps him know he's expected to help and not play second fiddle; it also helps him feel that he's an

important part of loving his sister or brother and meeting the baby's needs, just as you are.

Make realistic getting-along goals.
Don't expect your child to smother the new baby with as much tenderness as you do. He may be older, but don't forget that he has needs and wants to be fulfilled, too.

Plan time alone with each of your children.
Even if you have a half-dozen under-six-year-olds to attend to, try to plan time alone for you and each one (for example, a bath, walk, trip to the grocery store). This helps you focus your attention on a single child and his needs, and it lets you be aware of feelings and problems that may not surface amid the roar of the crowd at home.

Make individual brag boards (for parents of twins or children close in age).
Display each child's creativity in his own special place to reassure your child that it merits individual attention.

SOLVING THE PROBLEM

(WHAT TO DO)

Play Beat-the-Clock.
When your children are fighting among each other for your undivided attention, for example, let the timer determine when it's each child's turn to be held. This lets you be shared and lets each child know he will have a turn to be your number one object of attention, just like his brothers and sisters.

Offer alternatives to fighting.
Allowing fighting to flare up and continue to burn around your house doesn't teach children how to get along. Instead of allowing wars to be fought, give children a choice about what they can do when they're battling with each other—get along or not get along. Say, "You may get along with each other and continue to play, or not get along and be separated in Time Out." (See page 8 for more on Time Out.) Let them get in the habit of making choices to give them a feeling of control over their lives and to help them learn to make decisions on their own.

Define getting along.
Be specific in praising children when they are playing nicely together to make sure your children know what you mean by getting along. Say, "That's great that you're sharing and playing together so nicely. I really like how you're getting along so well—it makes playing together fun."

Don't respond to tattling.

Children tattle on each other as a way of enhancing their position with their parents. This game of one-upmanship can be stopped by your saying, "I'm sorry you aren't getting along!" and pretending that the tattling didn't occur. Even if a dangerous activity has been reported, you can stop the activity as you ignore the tattling itself.

Don't set up one child to tattle on another.

Asking big brother to come tell you when baby sister is doing something, for example, is not a good way to teach your children how to get along without tattling.

Don't get upset when your children don't love each other all the time.

Due to human nature, children cannot live in the same home without some rivalry existing between them. Keep friction to a minimum by rewarding getting along and not allowing the rivalry to become war.

Don't hold grudges.

After the fighting's settled, don't remind your children that they used to be enemies in the war. Start over with a clean slate.

"STARR" WARS

The constant warfare between four-year-old Jason Starr and his two-year-old sister, Julie, made their mom and dad feel like referees, roles that made them wonder why they ever had children—particularly ones who didn't appreciate all they sacrificed to buy them nice clothes, new toys, and good food.

Biting and teasing were two of Jason's favorite ways of letting his sister "have it" when he thought she was taking too much of his mother and father's time and attention away from him. Jason seemed to deliberately try to get yelled at and walloped—his punishments whenever he started hurting his sister.

The only time Mrs. Starr ever noticed her son being nice to his sister was when he helped her across an icy patch on the driveway. Mrs. Starr was so grateful for any bit of decency that she told her son, "That's great the way you are helping your sister. I'm really proud of you."

Later, the Starrs decided that to encourage more episodes like this they would try to dish out compliments when their children got along and figure out a new way to deal with their children when they fought.

They had a chance to put their new policy into practice when they got home from a shopping trip later that day and a battle over blocks began. Mrs. Starr had no idea who started the argument but told her children, "You have a choice now, kids; since I don't know who took the toy from whom, you can get along and play and talk like you did in the car today, or be separated in Time Out."

Neither child answered their mother's new question—they continued to play tug of war with the blocks. So Mrs. Starr followed with another new announcement: "You both have made the choice of going to Time Out," and she proceeded to put each of them in a Time-Out chair.

Julie and Jason screamed their way through the time limit, but after quieting down and being allowed to come out of their chairs, they had different looks on their faces for the rest of the day. They began to act like members of the same army instead of like enemies, and their mother was delighted that *she* had not lost her temper when her children had.

The Starrs continued to point out any time their children got along, putting less emphasis on any fighting they noticed, and they consistently used Time Out to separate the children and reinforce the consequences of choosing to fight.

TOILETING ACCIDENTS

Toilet training is the first major battle of wills between parents and preschoolers. The war breaks out when parents ask their independence-loving offspring to give up something that is second nature to them and to begin to do something that is new and often undesirable. To most children, what is desirable about toilet training is pleasing their parents; so to foster the least accident-prone toilet training possible, try to put more attention on what your child should do (keep her pants dry, go to the bathroom in the potty) than on what she shouldn't do (go potty in her pants). Help your child feel proud of herself while you lessen the likelihood that she will have an accident just to get your attention and reaction.

Note: If your child is having continuous toileting accidents after the age of four, consult a medical professional. This chapter does not discuss bedwetting because many preschoolers are simply not developmentally able to stay dry all night. Many authorities believe that after age six, bedwetting may be considered a problem to be dealt with in various ways.

PREVENTING THE PROBLEM

Look for signals that your child is ready for training (most children are ready somewhere around the age of two).

The generally accepted signs of readiness are: the ability to stay dry for a few hours at a time; to understand words like "potty," "wet," and "dry"; and to follow simple directions like "pull down your pants," "sit on the potty seat," etc.

Don't try training too early.

Early training simply teaches children to be more dependent on parents than on their own ability to manage toileting.

Model correct potty usage.

Familiarize your child with the potty and how it is used by showing her how you go to the bathroom and then how she can.

Make it as convenient as possible to potty where and when your child might need to.

Put the potty chair on the kitchen floor, for example, during basic training. Take your child's potty with you in the initial stages of potty training in order to help her feel comfortable about pottying in public.

Use a toilet training procedure and stick with it.

The one described in *Toilet Training in Less Than a Day*, for example, answers concerns and gives a step-by-step approach.

SOLVING THE PROBLEM

WHAT TO DO

Reward being dry as well as correct toileting.

Teach your child to keep herself dry by telling her how good staying dry is. This will help her emphasize the times she has done what you've expected of her (stay dry) and give that behavior more attention than she does mistakes. About every fifteen minutes say to your child, "Check your pants—are they dry?" This also makes the responsibility of checking on her dryness rest with your child, making her feel more in control of the matter. If she's dry, tell her you're glad. Say, "How nice that you are staying dry."

Remind your child of the rule for wrong places.

Many preschoolers will occasionally go to the bathroom in an inappropriate place (outside, for example). When your child has that experience, remind her that the rule is "You're supposed to potty in the potty. Let's practice." Then proceed in practicing correct pottying procedures.

React calmly to accidents.

Weight your toilet training efforts toward asking your child to practice how to stay dry by correctly toileting. This strengthens your child's self-confidence and shows her that she can toilet in the way you want her to. If your child is wet, say, "I'm sorry that you are wet. Now we need to practice staying dry." Then practice ten times going to the toilet from various parts of the house (pants down, sit on the toilet, pants up, sit on the toilet at the next station, etc.). In practice it's not necessary for your child to urinate or have a bowel movement, but only to go through correct toileting motions.

Remember, children don't always see a reason for toileting the way we want.

If being wet is not a problem for your child, emphasize the importance of dryness through rewards to help children recognize its benefits. Say, "You're such a big girl for keeping dry. Because you're staying dry, we can read a book now," for example.

Use Grandma's Rule in public.

When your child wants to only go in her potty when you are in public, enforce Grandma's Rule. Take your child's potty with you if you can, or offer incentives for using other people's potties, like, "We need to keep dry. One potty is the same as another. We can't use your potty because it's not here. When you've used this potty, we can go on a trip to the zoo."

WHAT NOT TO DO

Don't punish toileting accidents.

Punishment only gives your child attention for toileting in her pants or another wrong place and doesn't teach how to stay dry.

Don't ask the wrong question.

Saying "check your pants" frequently acts as a subtle reminder and is a good substitute for "Do you need to go potty?" a question generally answered no. Help your child feel responsible for checking her dry-wet condition and doing something about it to increase how grown up she feels because she's able to take care of herself like Mom and Dad.

KELLY'S "ACCIDENTS"

As soon as preschool let out for the summer, three-and-a-half-year-old Kelly Winter started to lose more than her knowledge of numbers and letters: her occasional toileting accidents signaled that it she was waiting too long before starting for the bathroom. Mrs. Winter would see her "dance" as she worked hard to avoid going to the bathroom.

Kelly found that she could relieve the physical pressure of having to "go" by releasing only a small amount of urine into her pants. When her mother would scold and spank her for wetting her pants, Kelly would point out how she just wet "a little."

Obviously, Mrs. Winter thought, Kelly wanted some attention for her accidents—why else would she point out when she was just a little wet?

After analyzing the situation, Mr. and Mrs. Winter decided to reinstate the routine they had used to toilet train their daughter the previous year, and they began to praise Kelly's dry pants instead of getting upset when she had wet ones.

"Check your pants, Kelly," Mrs. Winter ordered her the next morning after breakfast. "Are they dry?"

Mrs. Winter was as delighted as Kelly when her daughter happily replied "Yes!" with a big grin.

"Thanks for keeping yourself dry, honey," she praised her daughter, giving her a hug at the same time. "Let's keep them dry all day!"

When she had spent a few days encouraging Kelly to check her pants periodically (and when Kelly had found herself dry), Mrs. Winter thought her problem was behind her—until the very next day when Kelly was wet again.

"Let's practice ten times going to the potty," she told her glum-looking daughter, who seemed very disappointed that her mother was not praising her as she did when the pants were dry.

Soon Kelly learned that it was easier to go to the potty and get the praise for dry pants than it was to practice going for ten times, and she continued to follow through with keeping her pants dry for several months.

Mr. and Mrs. Winter had to praise Kelly and remind her several times during the next year. They kept in mind that Kelly had to firmly reestablish the right way of toileting and that was a job that her parents would rather help her do than become angry and frustrated when she soiled her pants.

CLINGING TO PARENTS

The image of a child clutching his mother's skirt, hanging on for dear life while she tries to cook or walk out the door, is not an imaginary one for many parents of clinging preschoolers—it's a very real and emotionally draining part of daily life. Though tough to resist, don't give in to the temptation to stay home or play with a clinging vine as you go about the task of living your life. If you want or need to leave your child with a babysitter, arm him with firm, loving reassurance that you're proud of him for playing alone and that you will return, and tell him in a sincere voice that you are happy he has the chance to play with the babysitter. Your positive attitude will be contagious (as would a negative one) and will provide a model for feeling okay about being separated from you and having a good time in the process of independence. Providing your child with armfuls of hugs and kisses during neutral times helps prevent him from feeling ignored and clinging to you to get attention. Clinging differs from hugging—it's an immediate, urgent demand for attention.

PREVENTING THE PROBLEM

Practice leaving your child at an early age.
To get your child used to the idea that you may not always be around, practice leaving him occasionally for short periods of time (a few hours) early in his life.

Tell your child what you'll both be doing in your absence.
Telling your child what you'll be doing when you are gone gives him a good example to follow when you ask him to talk about his day's activities. Describe what he'll be doing and where you will be while

you're away from each other so he won't worry about your fate or his. Say, for example, "Laura will fix your dinner, read you a story, and then you'll go to bed. Your daddy and I are going out to dinner, and we'll be back at eleven o'clock tonight." Or say, for example, "I need to cook dinner now. When I've done that and you've played with Play-Doh, then we can read a story together."

Play peekaboo.

This simple game gets your child used to the idea that things (and you) go and, most important, come back. One- through five-year-olds play peekaboo in a variety of ways— by hiding behind their hands, watching others hide behind their fingers, and (for two- to five-year-olds in particular), engaging in a more physically active game of hide-and-seek.

Reassure your child that you will be coming back.

Don't forget to tell him that you will be returning—and prove to him you're as good as your word by coming back when you said you would.

Provide activities that your child only gets to do when you're away or busy.

Prepare your child for the separation.

Plant the suggestion that you are leaving and that your child can cope while you're gone by saying, "I know you're such a big boy and that you'll be fine while I'm gone." If you surprise him by leaving without warning, he may always wonder when you're going to disappear suddenly again.

SOLVING THE PROBLEM

WHAT TO DO

Prepare yourself for noise when you separate and your child doesn't like it.

Remember that the noise will only subside when your child learns the valuable lesson that he can survive without you for a brief time. Say to yourself, "I know that his crying is letting me know that he loves me. He needs to learn that though I don't play with him or may go away, I will always be back again and will play soon."

Praise your child when you've separated.

Make your child proud of his abilities to play by himself. Say, "I'm so proud of you for entertaining yourself while I clean the oven," for example. "You are really grown-up." This will make his time away from you hold more benefits from both of your points of view.

Use the whining chair.

Let your child know that it is okay for him not to like your being busy or leaving him, but that whining is disturbing to others. Say, "I'm sorry that you don't like my having to cook dinner now. Go to the whining chair until you can play without whining." (See Whining, pages 39 to 42.) Let a crying child cry—away from you.

Recognize that your child needs some time with and without you.
Breaks from being together day in and day out are necessary for both children and parents. So persist in your daily routine, even if your child protests your doing something besides play with him or fusses when you leave him with a babysitter occasionally.

Start separations slowly.
If your child demands too much of your time from age one and up, play Beat-the-Clock. Give him five minutes of your time and five minutes to play by himself. Keep increasing the play-by-himself time for each five minutes of your time until your child can play for one hour by himself.

WHAT NOT TO DO

Don't become upset when your child clings.
Assume you are more comfortable to be with than the big world and your child prefers your company.

Don't punish your child for clinging.
Teach him how to separate by using the timer.

Don't give mixed messages.
Don't tell your child to go away while holding, patting, or stroking him. This confuses your child about whether he should stay or go.

Don't make sickness a reason for breaking routine.
Make sure you don't make getting sick more fun than being well by letting your child do things when he's sick that are usually unacceptable. Research in adult pain management indicates that children who receive considerable special attention while sick are far less able to manage chronic pain when they become adults. Sickness should be dealt with in a matter-of-fact way with few routine changes.

"DON'T LEAVE ME!"

Joan and Rick Gordon loved the party circuit so much that when their four-year-old son, Paul, clutched both their jackets in horror when a babysitter arrived, both parents discounted his feelings.

"Oh come on, Paul, honey, don't be a baby! We love you—it's silly for you to feel bad. We go out every Saturday," they explained as they kissed their son good-bye one night on their way out.

But Paul wasn't comforted, and he screamed his well-rehearsed lines at top volume: "Don't go! Don't leave! Take me!" he cried.

The Gordons couldn't understand what they were doing wrong to make their son "punish" them whenever they wanted to leave the house. Did he hate them that much, they asked themselves, to embarrass them in front of his babysitter and stain their party clothes with sticky clutching fingers?

When they picked up their friends, the Reillys, and related their frustration, their friends tried to reassure them by explaining that it was because their son loved them so much, not hated them, that Paul clung to their security. They then told them how they had helped *their* daughter adjust to their absence.

The Gordons tried the Reillys' strategy the very next Saturday night. Before they left, they prepared Paul for their upcoming exit, saying, "I know you're such a big boy that you'll be just fine while we're gone to the movies. We will be back after you're in bed, but we'll be here in our bed in the morning when you awake. Laura will make you popcorn in our new popcorn maker, read you a story, and then you'll go to bed. Have fun!" They didn't drag out their exit over tearful hugs, but left while Paul was only whimpering.

After this apparent success, each time the Gordons left the house, they gave their son plenty of praise about how quiet he was being while they explained where they were going, what they were going to do, and how long they would be gone.

And when they got a good report about Paul from the babysitter, they would let him know the next day how proud they were of him for playing nicely while they were gone. "Thanks for being so calm and for helping Laura make the krispy treats last night," they would comment with a hug.

The Gordons were patient, knowing they might have to wait several weeks before they could expect to be able to leave the house to the sounds of happy feet, not stomping and wailing. In the meantime, they didn't verbally attack Paul for any babyish behavior, and by ignoring his crying they helped to erase its purpose.

INTERACTING WITH STRANGERS

"Don't take candy from strangers" is an admonition millions of parents of preschoolers dish out to their young ones every time they venture from home without them. The warning is a valid one. Children need to learn how to behave in general with strangers, just as they need to know how to interact with people with whom they are expected to socialize. Minimize the fear your child has of strangers by teaching her how to differentiate between saying hello and going with strangers, or following a stranger's suggestions, for instance. Soon your child will have the security of knowing what to do when you're there and when you're not.

PREVENTING THE PROBLEM

Establish the rules.

Let your child know your rules about interacting with strangers. A basic rule could be: "You may only say hello or no to people you don't know. If a stranger asks you to go with him or tries to give you anything, say no and run to the nearest house and ring the doorbell."

Practice following the rules.

Pretend you are a stranger and ask your child to run to the nearest house to familiarize your child with following your directions concerning strangers.

Don't try to frighten your child.

Fear only breeds confusion and doesn't teach your child what to do. She needs to know how to think on her feet when strangers invade her privacy. Being fearful on a grand scale will destroy her ability to behave rationally.

SOLVING THE PROBLEM

WHAT TO DO

Remind your child of the rule by praising correct behavior.
If your child says hello to a stranger while you are present, tell her you approve of her following the rule. Say, "I'm so glad you remembered only to say hello. Remember, that's the only thing you say to them."

Encourage your child to be friendly.
Friendly children tend to be more readily accepted by others as they go through life, so teaching friendliness is important. It's important to differentiate (for young and older children) what, when, and how friendliness should be transmitted.

Model friendliness.
Show your child the proper way to be friendly by saying hello to people, even strangers you meet on the street. Trying to teach children how to differentiate between strangers who are potentially dangerous and those who aren't is impossible. Even adults are often fooled by "normal-looking" criminals. Add to each of your lessons some words about how to be friendly without going with strangers or taking their offers of candy, gifts, etc.

WHAT NOT TO DO

Don't instill fear of people.
To help your child avoid the danger of being molested, teach her the rule; do not teach her to fear people. Fear only inhibits correct decision-making, regardless of age.

Don't worry about your child bothering others by saying hello.
Even if a person doesn't acknowledge the greeting, it is good for your child to have offered a salutation at the correct time and place.

KEEPING KEVIN SAFE

How can we teach our three-and-a-half-year-old son, Kevin, to be friendly yet keep him safe? That was the challenge Mr. and Mrs. Docking faced in trying to solve the problem of their friendly son always saying "hi" to absolute strangers on the street. What if he did more than say "hi" to the wrong audience?, they worried, silently.

"Some day someone may take advantage of your friendliness," they explained to little Kevin, using adult logic. "Do not talk to strangers," they firmly ordered, when their first logical explanation did not deter his unrestricted friendliness.

Kevin listened so intently to their adamant orders to keep to himself, that he became terrified and began to throw tantrums every time his parents wanted him to go to shopping centers or grocery stores where strangers lurked. He did not want to see strangers, he explained to his mother. They were so mean and dangerous that he couldn't even say "hello" to them.

Mrs. Docking was frustrated to see her well-meant ways of protecting her son backfire this way. She finally realized that Kevin didn't understand the difference between saying "hello," which they didn't want to squelch, and *going* with strangers or *taking things* from them, which the Dockings really wanted to prevent. He didn't understand because she had never given him the chance to understand.

"Strangers may mean danger if you go places with them or take things from them," she stated specifically to her son. "The new rule, then," she continued, "is that you can talk to anyone you want, but if they give you something or want you to go somewhere with them, refuse the goods and offer and go to the nearest house or the nearest adult in a store." The two practiced this rule by going to a shopping center and running through Kevin's actions, with his mother playing the "stranger."

Feeling more secure in her son's ability, she reminded her son of the rule on a weekly basis until Mrs. Docking realized that it was now part of Kevin's habit, not just an odd way of navigating through the world. To reinforce the lesson, Mrs. Docking practiced saying "hello" to others, too, something that her son pointed out to her and praised her for, just as she praised him for following the rule.

The problem never completely disappeared from Mr. and Mrs. Docking's minds. They realized that they must encourage Kevin to practice "safe greetings" from time to time to convince them that he understood and remembered this potentially life-saving habit.

WANDERING AWAY IN PUBLIC

Curious little preschoolers make mental lists of what to see and do at shopping centers, grocery stores, etc., just as their parents do on paper. Chaos breaks out when the two lists don't match—and the preschoolers think their lists take priority. Knowing that your child's safety takes precedence over his curiosity in dangerous situations (his getting in the way of cars, pedestrians, or grocery carts, for example), enforces your instructions on how he must behave, despite protests against them. Make staying close in public a habit for your child until both of you safely rely on him to know what is and isn't dangerous—a distinction he'll have learned from you.

Note: To foster your child's staying close in public, your emphasis must be on preventing the misbehavior. Once your child has wandered away in public, the only thing to do is find him and prevent his wandering away again, before the lost condition becomes permanent.

PREVENTING THE PROBLEM

Establish rules for behaving in public.

At a neutral time (before or long after he misbehaves), let your child know what you expect from him in public. Say, "When we are in the store, you must stay one arm's length from me," for example.

Practice ahead of time.

So your child knows how to follow your rules, practice before leaving the house. Say, "We're going to try staying at arm's length. See how long you can stay close." After he does it, say, "Good staying close. Thanks for not moving away from me."

Teach your child to come to you.

During a neutral time, take your child's hand, say, "Come here, please!" and draw him to you. Give him a hug and say, "Thank you for coming." Practice five times a day, slowly increasing the distance your child is away from you when you say, "Come here, please!" until he can come to you from across the room or across the shopping center.

Praise staying close.

Make it worth your child's while to stay close by praising him every time he does. Say, "Good staying close," or "You are being such a good shopper by staying close to me," for example.

Let your child participate in the staying-close routine.

If he can, let your child hold a package or push the stroller, for example. This will make him feel he's an important part of the shopping procedure and less tempted to roam.

Change your rule as your child changes.

As your child matures and becomes able to walk away briefly and come right back to your side in a shopping center, for instance, you might change your rule. Tell him why you are giving him more freedom, making him feel that he earned that independence by good behavior in public. This will help him realize the rewards of following rules.

Be firm and consistent.

Don't change your public behavior rules without first telling your child. Being firm and consistent will give your child a sense of security. Knowing his limits may produce some yelling and screaming, but the safety check you provide will help him feel protected in foreign territory.

SOLVING THE PROBLEM

(WHAT TO DO)

Use reprimands and Time Out.

Reprimanding your child for not staying close in public will teach him what behavior you want and what will happen to him if he doesn't follow your rule. When you see him not staying close, say, "No, don't wander away. You're supposed to stay with me. Staying close to me keeps you safe." If he repeatedly breaks your rule, restate the reprimand and put him in Time Out immediately (in a corner of the store or a nearby chair) while you stay with him.

Don't let your child dictate your chores.

Don't threaten to go home if your child doesn't stay close. Going home may be just what he prefers, so he might wander away just to get his wish granted.

Don't spank your child in public.

This only encourages him to move away from you because he isn't sure when you will punish him and when you won't.

Don't take your child shopping for longer than he can tolerate.

Some preschoolers can follow rules for longer periods of time than others. Get to know your child. One hour may be the longest time, so consider that before you leave home.

STAYING PUT

Mr. and Mrs. Brody could not comfortably take their four-year-old son, Matthew, to a shopping center or grocery store anymore—he was always wandering out of sight as soon as his parents turned their backs.

"Stay here! Never run away when we are shopping!" Mrs. Brody screamed at her son the last time he disappeared under a lingerie rack at the department store.

Her order proved ineffective; as they left the store and strolled down the mall, Matthew ran ten feet away toward a store window, pointing and screaming, "Look at that train! Look at that train!"

The shop window was almost out of hearing range, panicking Mrs. Brody who then realized that some rules needed to be set to prevent her son from disappearing while she did her holiday shopping that year. The next morning, before they went to the grocery store, she explained the new rule to her son, because she knew that the grocery store was his favorite place to race from aisle to aisle.

"Matthew, you must stay within an arm's length of me at all times," she began. "As long as you stay that close, you may look at things with your eyes, not with your hands!"

During their trial run, Matthew was out of sight in minutes. "Do not wander away," Mrs. Brody told him when she finally caught up with him in Aisle 3 and pulled him close. "You're supposed to stay with me at an arm's length. Staying close to me keeps you safe."

Matthew had never heard this lecture before and wasn't sure how important it was. He acted like he didn't hear it then, taking off toward the granola bars he so loved.

Mrs. Brody, who was boiling inside but cool on the surface, told herself that the rules were new, and, like all rules, they would need practice before they would be followed perfectly.

"You are supposed to stay with me because staying close keeps you safe," she said, repeating the reprimand to her son. She then walked him to the quiet corner by the produce and turned her back on him while staying near.

Matthew glared at his mother in protest, yelling, "No! I want to play. I don't like you!" His tantrum was ignored by his embarrassed but unflinching mother, who had decided that if a reprimand did not solve this problem her son would be put in Time Out to help him learn the rule.

At the end of three minutes (which seemed like three hours to Mrs. Brody), she greeted Matthew with a smile and reviewed the rule as they finished the shopping together. Whenever Matthew stayed within range, Mrs. Brody praised him. "Thanks for staying close, honey. I'm really glad that we're shopping together," she added as they began to talk about cereals and planned which one to buy for the next day's breakfast.

By consistently reprimanding him, Mrs. Brody rarely had to use Time Out in the next few weeks because Matthew and she were having too much fun enjoying the new closeness between them.

DEMANDING TO DO THINGS THEMSELVES

"Let me do it myself" is one of the lines parents of preschoolers can expect to hear as soon as their child's second birthday has come and gone. This declaration of independence marks the beginning of parents' golden opportunity to let practice make perfect for young try-it-alls, as long as the rules of the household are not infringed during the trial-and-error period. Because the ultimate goal of child-rearing is for children to be self-confident and self-sufficient, let your patience level soar as you bear with mistakes and balance the need to get chores done with the importance of teaching your preschoolers living skills.

PREVENTING THE PROBLEM

Don't assume your child can't do something.
Keep track of your child's changing levels of expertise. Make sure you've given her a chance to try something before you take over doing it, so you don't underestimate her current ability.

Buy clothing that your child can manage.
Buy clothes that easily go up and down for your child in potty training, for example. Buy shirts that will go over her head and not get stuck on her shoulders when she puts on her own clothes.

Store clothing in coordinated units.
Help your child develop an eye for coordination by sorting her clothes to make them easier for her (and you) to reach.

Forecast frustration.
Try to make tasks as easy for your child to accomplish as possible. Undo

the snaps on her pants or start the zipper on a coat before you let your child finish the job, for example.

SOLVING THE PROBLEM

Play Beat-the-Clock.

Tell your child how much time you have for a certain activity so she won't think it's her inability to do something that makes you take over the job. Set a timer for the number of minutes you want to allow for the task and say, "Let's see if we can get dressed before the timer rings," for example. This also helps children learn a sense of being on time and reduces the power struggle between you and your child because you will not be telling her to do something, the timer will. If you're in a hurry and must finish a task your child is beginning, explain your haste to your child, instead of letting her think it was her slow try at the job that's making you take over.

Suggest cooperation/sharing.

Because your child is not aware of why she cannot do something or that she will be able to soon, suggest that you share the job of dressing or eating, for example, by having you do the part that's too difficult for her to perform at her age (tie shoes for a one-year old, for example). Say, "Why don't you hold your sock and I'll put on your shoe," to let your child accomplish something, not just watch you and feel inadequate.

Make effort count.

As her favorite teacher, you can encourage your child to attempt tasks. You know that practice makes perfect, so teach your child this axiom by saying, for example, "I like the way you tried to braid your hair. That was a great try. We'll do it again later, too." Find something good about bad performance. Praise your child's try at putting on her shoes, even if she did it incorrectly.

Remain as calm as you can.

If your child wants you to do nothing and her to do everything ("I'll put on my shorts." "I'll open the door." "Me close the drawer."), remember that she is beginning to assert her independent side, not her obstinate one. Since you want her ultimately to do things by herself, let her try. Though you may not want to wait or put up with her incorrect drawer closing or napkin placement, for example, don't get upset when things are not done as quickly or precisely as you'd like. Try to be delighted that your child is taking the first step toward being self-sufficient and be proud of her for taking the initiative.

Allow as much independence as possible.

Try to allow your child to do as much as she can by herself, so frustration won't replace her inborn sense of curiosity. Let her hold her other shoe and give it to you, for example, instead of insisting upon keeping it away from her fidgety fingers while you tie her first shoe.

Ask your child to do things, don't demand.

To make your preschooler more likely to ask for things nicely, show how to make requests politely. Say, "When you ask me nicely, I'll let you do X." Then explain what you mean by "nicely." Tell your child to say, "Please, may I get a fork," when she wants a fork, for example.

WHAT NOT TO DO

Don't punish your child's mistakes.

If she wants to pour the milk herself and it spills, for instance, remind yourself to help her do it the next time. Remember, practice makes perfect; don't expect success right away.

Don't criticize your child's effort.

If it doesn't seem important to you, don't point out the mistake your child made. Even though her sock is on inside out, for instance, simply say, "Let's put the smooth side of the sock inside next to your foot, okay?" and drop it.

Don't feel rejected.

If your child says, "Let me open the door," and you know very well that you can do it faster and with less effort, don't let your child know that. Let her try to be independent and feel like you're appreciative of how she does things. Don't feel hurt because your child doesn't appreciate your help—know that your child is growing up, and that is as it should be.

INDEPENDENT JUDY

During the first three years of Judy Manning's life, her mother did everything for her. Now "Miss Independence" (as her mother called her) wanted her mother to do *nothing* for her, a personality change that was confusing and frustrating for Mrs. Manning.

"I can't stand waiting for you, Judy!" she told her when they were late for preschool and Judy refused to let her mother help put her coat on. "You can't do it," her mother continued to explain to convince her daughter not to do things beyond her years.

The waves of demanding and refusing to comply shifted just when Mrs. Manning felt the problem was causing her to dislike Judy as well as hate her desire to do things herself. As her daughter was dressing to go outside one morning, Mrs. Manning noticed Judy putting on her coat, completing the job perfectly by herself for the first time. "That's great the way you put on your coat," Mrs. Manning complimented her, starting to zip up the coat for her. "You're really hurrying to get ready for school! I'm so proud of you," her mother added. They walked out the door after Judy let her mother finish the job without putting up a fight for the first time in weeks.

As they rode to school, Mrs. Manning thought about how independent her daughter was getting at preschool, according to her teacher, wanting to answer questions and be "the helper" without being told.

Mrs. Manning decided she would try to tolerate Judy's willingness to be self-sufficient, something she had so longed for in Judy a year ago, tempering her allowance of independence with a timer, a mechanism that helped Judy get ready for bed and accept sharing her toys.

The next day Judy wanted to set the table by herself, as usual. Instead of helping her, Mrs. Manning announced the new timer plan. "Judy, you can try to set the table yourself until the timer rings. When it goes off, it's time for me to help you. Let's see if you can set the table before the timer rings."

Judy wasn't eager for her mother's assistance, but she loved the idea of beating the timer and was extra proud of herself that night for completing the job before the bell sounded.

Judy's mother was proud, too. "That's great the way you set the table all by yourself," she remarked, as she silently shifted the spoons to their place beside, not inside, the bowls (but not mentioning it to her daughter).

Judy's mother continued to praise her daughter's efforts at any stroke of independence when it was appropriate, making it as easy as possible for her to complete tasks, and both of them began jointly finishing jobs, when necessary.

DEMANDING FREEDOM

Immersed in pushing their way out into the world, preschoolers may need to be pulled back to safety because they're not as self-sufficient, self-reliant, and self-controlled as they think. As your one-year-old grows, your apron strings will gradually stretch to accommodate him. Let him go only as far as you know is safe. Get to know your child's limits by testing his maturity and responsibility before you make the mistake of allowing more freedom than he can happily handle.

Note: Remember to allow freedoms that are commensurate with your child's ability—constantly giving him opportunities to reinforce your belief that he's mature enough to handle the freedom you're allowing him.

PREVENTING THE PROBLEM

Decide family freedom limits.
Your child needs to know his limits—what he can and can't do, when he is allowed to go, etc.—before he should be expected to do what you want him to do. Let even a one-year-old know what's "legal" territory to prevent as many "illegal" actions as possible.

Let your child know when he can cross the boundaries.
Lessen the lure some no-no's have just because they are off-limits by showing and telling your young adventurer how he can do what he wants and not get in trouble for it. Say, "You can cross the street only when you are holding my hand," for example.

Allow as much freedom as your child shows he can safely handle.
If your child shows he is responsible within the limits, extend them a little. Let him know why they've changed to help him feel good about his

ability to follow directions and be responsible enough to earn freedom. Say, "Because you always tell me before you go to your friend's house next door, you can now go up the street, too; always ask me before you go, of course."

SOLVING THE PROBLEM

WHAT TO DO

Offer rewards for staying within limits.

Make it more pleasant for your child to stay within the limits by piling on the attention when your child is being good. Say, "I'm so glad that you stayed at the swingset and didn't go into the neighbor's yard. You can swing for three more minutes now!"

Restrict freedoms.

Teach your child that not heeding the limits brings his fun to a stop. Say, "I'm sorry you left the yard; now you must stay in the house." Or, "I'm sorry you crossed the street; now you must only play in the backyard."

Be as consistent as you can.

Don't let your child break a rule without enforcing the consequences to teach him that you mean what you say every time you say it. This will also help him feel more secure about his actions once he's on his own because he'll already have learned what you expect him to do.

WHAT NOT TO DO

Don't spank your child for going into the street.

Spanking encourages your child to hide from you while he's still doing what you punished him for. Children who sneak out in the street are in great danger, of course, so don't add to the problem by making your preschooler want to do it on the sly.

SALLY ON HER OWN

Five-year-old Sally Hamilton was the most popular little girl on Twelfth Street, a fact that also caused her to be the biggest problem in the Hamilton family of seven children.

"I have to walk to school with Susie, go to Donna's house after lunch, and play dolls with Maria today," Sally informed her mother at breakfast one morning.

When her mother told her that she could not go anywhere anytime she pleased that day or any day, Sally pleaded, "Why? Why not? I'm going anyway—you can't stop me!"

These kinds of rebellious statements encouraged angry name-calling episodes between Sally and her parents, particularly after Sally darted alone across the street to her best friend's house one day, even though she was not allowed to cross the street by herself.

Screaming, "It's not fair," Sally was sent to her room that day by her frustrated parents, who could not decide where freedom should be given and boundaries drawn to protect their "baby" daughter from dangers she was not old enough to handle. Because she was constantly getting invitations, they could not ignore the problem of deciding where and when Sally could go.

To solve the problem, the Hamiltons finally decided to reach a compromise between themselves and their daughter—and establish rules for freedom that they could change as their daughter proved she was responsible enough to warrant it. They began by explaining these new rules to their daughter, who was more than happy to learn how to get more freedom.

"I want you to learn how to cross the street, Sally," her mother told her when Sally asked if she could visit her friend in the gold house.

Sally and her mother went to the curb where Mrs. Hamilton began to teach street-crossing behavior—how to stop at the curb, look to the left, look to the right, and not only *look* but also *see*. Mrs. Hamilton asked her daughter to describe what she saw to the left and right. Once she made sure the street was cleared, she instructed her daughter to cross the street only while holding her hand. Then they crossed the street together, looking right and left, describing what they saw. After ten practices, with Mrs. Hamilton praising her daughter for following the directions perfectly, she said, "Sally, let me watch you cross the street on your own."

When Sally had shown that she could follow the rules, Mrs. Hamilton announced the new rule: "You may cross the street to go to your friend's, but you must first come and tell me, and I will come with you to watch you."

This compromise was a lot of work, thought Mrs. Hamilton, but she realized that the only way she would feel comfortable with loosening her apron strings was if she knew her daughter could handle the responsibilities the freedom required. Establishing and then practicing the conditions of freedom let everyone feel satisfied and secure with the limits and expectations.

WANTING THEIR OWN WAY

Because patience is not an innate virtue of human beings, young children must be taught the art of waiting for what they want to do, see, eat, touch, or hear. Because you are more experienced in knowing what's best for your preschooler, you're more qualified to control when she can do what she wants and what she must do before she does it. While dishing out that control, explain to your one- to five-year-old when and how she can get what she wants. Also, show how having patience pays off in your life, too. Say, for instance, "I know it's unpleasant for me to wait to buy the new dining room furniture I want, but I know that if I work hard at saving money, I will be able to buy it soon." Or say, "I know you want to eat the cake batter, but you don't need it now; and if you wait until it is baked, it will turn into more cake for you to eat." She is just discovering that the world will not always revolve around her wants and desires. It's not too soon for her to start learning the skills to cope with that often frustrating fact of life.

PREVENTING THE PROBLEM

Provide a menu of activities from which your child may choose.
Set up conditions under which your child gets her own way, and provide your child with suggestions for what she can do while she's waiting to do what she wants to do. Say, "When you've played with the pegs for five minutes, then we'll go to Grandma's," for example.

SOLVING THE PROBLEM

Encourage patience.

Reward even the slightest sign of patience by telling your child how glad you are that she waited or did a chore, for example. Define patience for your child if you feel that patience might be a word she's not familiar with. Say, for example, "You are being so patient by waiting calmly for your drink until I clean the sink. That shows me how grown-up you are." This teaches your child that she *does* have the ability to put off her wants, even though she doesn't know it yet; it also makes her feel good about herself because you feel good about her behavior.

Remain as calm as you can.

If your child protests waiting or not having things her own way, remind yourself that she is learning a valuable lesson for living—the art of being patient. By seeing you be patient, she'll soon learn that demanding doesn't get her wants satisfied as fast as getting the job done does.

Let your child participate in the process of getting to do things—use Grandma's Rule.

If your child is screaming to go! go! go! to Grandma's, for example, use the conditions you've set up ahead of time about what your child must do before she gets to do what she wants. This increases the likelihood that she will do the chore in store for her. State the conditions in a positive way. Say, "When you've put the books back in the bookshelf, we will go to Grandma's," for example.

Avoid saying a flat no to what your child wants.

Tell your child how she can have her own way (when it's possible and safe), instead of letting her feel that her wants are never going to be satisfied. Say, for example, "When you've washed your hands, then you may have an apple." Sometimes, of course, you need to say no to your child (when she wants to play with your lawnmower, for instance). At these times, try to offer alternative playthings to fulfill your child's wishes and foster a sense of compromise and flexibility in your child.

Don't demand that your child do something "now."

Demanding that your child does what you want this instant only gives credence to the idea that she should always have her own way immediately, just as you want things your own way immediately.

Don't reward impatience.

Don't give in to what your child wants every time she wants her own way. Although it's tempting to put off what you're doing to satisfy your child and avoid a battle or tantrum, giving her her own way when she's demanding it only teaches her not to learn patience and increases the likelihood of her continuing to want her own way immediately and always.

Make sure your child knows it's not the demanding that got her wants fulfilled.

Though your child may moan and groan throughout the waiting time, make sure she knows that you're getting in the car because you're ready and your jobs are done, not because she wailed her way out the door. Say, "I've finished washing the dishes. We can go now."

"I WANT IT NOW!"

"**D**rink now," two-year-old Emily Randolph wailed every time she was thirsty. When she saw her mother giving a bottle to her new baby brother, Justin, she wanted one, too—immediately.

"No, I'm busy. You'll just have to wait!" her mother responded, beginning to get impatient with her daughter for not understanding that babies didn't know how to wait for what they wanted like big girls.

Emily made so many demands to be held or be given toys or drinks that Mrs. Randolph dreaded the moment when Emily would enter the room at the same time she was busy with anything, and especially when she was satisfying one of Justin's needs.

When Emily began taking food, drink, toys, and blankets away from Justin, saying they were "mine," Mrs. Randolph realized that they needed to start controlling this problem. She declared a new rule she called Grandma's Rule, and explained it to Emily: "When you do what I ask you to do, you may do what you want to do," she told her. "That is the new rule around here."

That afternoon, when Emily insisted on having a drink only ten minutes after the last one, Mrs. Randolph stated firmly, "When you have put on your shoes, you may have some apple juice."

Emily was used to hearing a "no," and then throwing a tantrum until her mother screamed, "Okay, okay," and gave in to letting her have her own way. She ignored her mother's new rule and began to plead, "I'm thirsty! I'm thirsty!" as usual.

Not only did her tantrum not bring a drink, it caused Mrs Randolph to ignore Emily completely. The frustrated little girl put on her shoes to see if *that* would bring her attention (and a drink) since screaming had not, and was surprised and delighted that it did.

She quickly learned that her mother meant what she said because Mrs. Randolph never changed her enforcement of the Grandma's Rule. As her daughter fulfilled her part of the bargain, Mrs. Randolph praised her accomplishments with comments like, "I'm so glad that you cleared the dishes from the table. You can go outside now."

She was sincere in her admiration of Emily's actions and her daughter seemed to appreciate that and become more responsive to her mother's demands, which Mrs. Randolph tried to limit when possible. As the family learned to work together to get their own way, they again enjoyed living with, not in spite of, each other.

Dawdling

Because time has no meaning to a child under six years old, hurrying has no great advantages. Disguise urging your child to "come on" or "please hurry" by running races with him or giving him chances to run to your arms, for example. Turn instructions into fun, not frustrating orders. Let your child still feel he's in control of how slow or fast he does things, then he won't need to dawdle just to exert his influence over the pace of things.

Preventing the Problem

Try to allow lead time.

If you're in a hurry, waiting for your preschool tortoise will often lead to your losing your cool and being that much later. Make every effort to allow enough time to get ready for outings, understanding that dawdling is a typical response to movement by someone who doesn't understand what hurrying means and is a full-time world investigator.

Maintain a routine time schedule.

Since a child needs routine and consistency in his day and tends to dawdle more when his routine is broken, establish time limits and a regular pattern of eating, moving from the car, etc., to familiarize your child with the time schedule on which you want him to operate.

Don't dawdle yourself.

Getting a child ready to go somewhere only to have him wait for you tells him that time is not important. Don't announce that you're ready to go to Grandma's house, for example, when you're not.

SOLVING THE PROBLEM

Make it easy for your child to move at your pace.

Play simple games to disguise hurrying, like having your child guess what Grandma's got in her house, to encourage his interest in getting going faster. Try asking your child to "run to your arms" if you want him to hurry along the path to your car, for example.

Play Beat-the-Clock.

Children always move more quickly while trying to beat the timer (a neutral authority) instead of trying to do what you ask. Say, "Let's see if you can get dressed before the timer rings," for example.

Offer incentives for speed.

Make these covert requests for hurrying have added benefit for your child. Say, "When you beat the timer, then you may play for ten minutes before we leave for school." This lets your child see for himself what good things come to those who stay on a time schedule.

Reward movement as well as result.

To spur your child on to completing a task, encourage him along the way. For example, say, "I like the way you are getting dressed so quickly," rather than only saying, "Thank you for getting dressed," after the fact.

Use manual guidance.

You may have to physically guide your child through the task at hand (getting in the car or dressing) to teach him that the world goes on, regardless of what his agenda is at the moment.

Use Grandma's Rule.

If your child dawdles when you have a pace to set for going somewhere or doing a task, for example, enforce Grandma's Rule. This will equate a quicker pace with his later getting to do what he wants to do. Say, "When you have finished getting dressed, then you may play with your train," for example.

Don't lose control.

If you're in a hurry and your child is not, don't slow both of you down even more by giving him attention for dawdling (nagging, or screaming at him to get going, for example). Getting angry will only encourage your child's easygoing pace.

Don't nag.
Nagging your child to hurry while he's dawdling only gives him attention while he is not moving rather than when he is. Disguise a hurry-up technique by turning it into a game.

DAWDLING ALLISON

Three-year old Allison repeatedly noticed grass blades or toyed with her shoestrings instead of doing what was necessary at the moment. Her Grandma Harris, the daily babysitter, felt bad about having to get angry and nearly drag her granddaughter to the door of preschool. "Hurry! Stop dawdling!" she would command, but Allison was oblivious to any encouragement to do anything faster than she wanted to do it.

Finally, Grandma Harris told her daughter that she could no longer care for Allison because she felt so helpless, angry, and resentful toward her favorite granddaughter. Mrs. Smith advised her mother to praise any of Allison's attempts at moving fast—giving her attention for not dawdling and ignoring her for wasting time—a technique she had to enforce with her daughter, too.

Grandma Harris also took her daughter up on her suggestion to offer Allison rewards for hurrying, something that came naturally for Grandma Harris, who was always bringing her grandchild presents.

"I'm glad that you're getting up and to the door ahead of me today," Grandma Harris said the next time Allison happened to walk down the block toward school more quickly than usual.

When Allison slowed down to her normal pace as they neared the school, Grandma Harris decided to encourage her speed, not complain about her dawdling. "When you've scurried up the walkway toward preschool before I can count to five, I'll give you that comb you saw in my purse," she told Allison, watching her granddaughter hustle as if she had never dawdled in her entire life.

Grandma Harris followed through with the comb and saw for herself the impact that rewards had on getting her granddaughter to do what she wanted her to.

Allison still had to be coaxed into dressing on her grandmother's, not her own, timetable, but now Grandma Harris was beginning to enjoy her grandchild again, and she felt in control of the time frame in which they would both operate.

NOT FOLLOWING DIRECTIONS

In daily fun and games, preschoolers are the world's greatest experts at testing how far parents' rules can be stretched, whether warnings will be enforced, and how closely directions must be followed. Consistently give your child the same results for her research about how the adult world works. Prove to her that you mean what you say, so she will feel more secure about what she can expect from other adults. Your being ultimately in control may sound like an unfair dictatorship to your child, but despite her protests she will be relieved that limits are set and rules defined as she moves from a little to a big person's world.

PREVENTING THE PROBLEM

Learn how many directions your child can follow at once.

Your preschooler will only be able to remember and then follow a certain number of directions at one time. To find out your child's limit, give one simple direction, then two, then three. For three directions, say, for example, "Please pick up the book, put it down on the table, and come sit by me." If all three are followed in the proper order, you'll know your child can remember three directions. If not, decide what her limit is and wait until she's older before giving more. Remember, only expect your child to follow the number of directions she can at a particular developmental stage.

Let your child do as many things by herself as possible without telling her to stop.

Because she wants to follow only her own directions and have total control over her life, your two-, three-, four-, or five-year-old will fight for the chance to make choices. Give her the opportunity to develop her decision-making skills and increase her self-confidence. The more control she feels she has, the less likely she'll be to reject taking directions from someone else.

Avoid unnecessary rules.

Analyze a rule's importance before you etch it in stone. Your preschooler needs as much freedom as possible to develop her independence, so let her have it.

Solving the Problem

What to do

Give simple, clear directions.

Being as specific as possible about what you want your child to do will make it easier for your child to follow directions. Make suggestions, but try not to criticize what she's done. Say, for example, "Please pick up your toys now and put them in the box," rather than "Why don't you ever remember to pick up your toys and put them away on your own?"

Praise following directions.

Reward your child for following your directions by showing her your pleasant reactions to a job well done. Teach her what to say when she appreciates what someone else has done, too, by saying, "Thank you for doing what I asked you to do," each time it's appropriate, as you would say to an adult friend.

Use countdown.

Make the rule that your child must start a task by the count of five, for example, to ease your child into the idea of leaving what she's enjoying doing for something you want her to do. Say, "Please pick up your toys now. Five-four-three-two-one." Thank your child for starting to clean up so quickly, if she does.

Comment about any progress along the way, not just when your directions have been completely followed.

Be a cheerleader as your child begins to make the right moves in the game you want her to play. Say, "That's great the way you're getting up and starting to put those toys away," for example.

Use Grandma's Rule for getting directions followed.

If your child can follow a direction, make doing a task worth a reward by saying, "When you have picked up the books, you may turn on the television," or "When you have washed your hands, we will have lunch."

Practice following directions.

If your child doesn't follow directions, practice by walking her through what you want her to do, guiding her manually, and praising and encouraging her. Say, "I'm sorry you weren't following directions. Now we have to practice." Practice five times, then give her the opportunity to follow directions on her own. If she still refuses, say, "Time out," and take her away from the situation.

WHAT NOT TO DO

Don't back down if your child resists.

Say to yourself, "I know my child doesn't want to do as I say, but I am more experienced and know what's best for her to do. I need to teach her by giving her clear directions, so she can eventually do things herself."

Don't punish your child for not following directions.

Teaching your child how to do something instead of showing her how mad you become when she doesn't do it saves your child's self-esteem from being hurt and puts less attention on bad behavior than on good.

"DO WHAT YOU'RE TOLD!"

Four-and-a-half-year-old Eric Jackson knew his alphabet and his numbers, and he was even starting to sound out words in his favorite books. The one thing he couldn't seem to do was the one thing his parents wanted most—follow their directions.

On a daily basis, his mother would ask things like, "Eric, please pick up your toys and then put your dirty clothes in the hamper," or "Come sit here on the couch and put on your boots, Eric."

Eric would get about halfway through the first task, then seem to lose track of what he was supposed to be doing and wanter off to investigate a toy truck or see what his brother was doing.

"How many times do I have to tell you what do do?" his frustrated mother yelled at him after one of these less-than-responsive sessions. "You never listen to me! You never understand what I tell you!" she continued, giving him a swift spanking for not complying with her wishes.

This continued until one day Eric shouted back, "I *can't* do what you want!" and his mother actually heard what he said and took his talk seriously. She decided to try one simple command and see if he could do what she wanted—any compliance would be better than none at all, she figured.

"Eric, please bring me your boots," she asked simply. As Eric marched right over to his blue and white boots, his mother clapped her hands in delight. "Thanks so much for doing what I asked you do do, Eric," she praised. "How nice to see you following my directions!"

She then gave Eric the next direction, to go get his coat on, and she again followed up with more praise and affection when he fulfilled her request.

Mrs. Jackson was delighted that she could stop threatening and screaming at her son and that by listening to Eric's feelings, she realized something that was crucial to their getting along. She continued to slowly increase the number of directions she gave her son, waiting until he had practiced doing two at a time, for example, before she gave him three at a time. Her clear language and promises of rewards like, "When you've put on your boots, you can go play in the snow for a minute before we go to Grandma's," helped her win the war against not following directions.

TRAVELING PROBLEMS

For most adults, traveling is a change of pace, scenery, and routine when cares of home are abandoned for the free and easy life. For the majority of preschoolers, though, traveling can be the exact opposite of a vacation because they thrive on the sense of security that their familiar toys, bed, and foods offer them day in and day out. Try to prevent your needing another vacation when you get home from one with your child by making sure your preschooler knows that his favorite things (toys, blankets, clothes) will be near and that he will be included in the fun (play games, take him to his favorite kinds of places). The comforts of home are often absent when you're traveling, so try teaching your child how to cope with change and how to enjoy new experiences—two tasks made easier if you have a happy, interested pupil who feels secure in his new surroundings.

Note: Remember that children who are not buckled in a safety restraint will continue to travel forward if a car stops suddenly. They will hit anything in their path—the dashboard, windshield, or back of the front seat—with the impact equivalent to a one-story drop for each ten miles per hour the car is traveling. Even though the dashboard and back of the front seat are padded, hitting them from five and one-half stories up (the impact you would have at fifty-five miles per hour) can still do considerable damage to small bodies. (See page 127 for more on car seat safety.)

PREVENTING THE PROBLEM

Check the car seat or seat restraints before traveling.
The safety measures you take before you leave will determine how relaxed you are with your children when take-off day arrives. Don't wait

until the last minute to find out you must delay your trip because you lack one of the most essential things to pack—the safety seat.

Practice the rule.

Before you and your child leave on a long-distance trip by car, take a few dry runs, so your child can graduate from basic training to the real thing. Praise any proper sitting in the car seat or seat belts during practice to show your child that staying in his car seat reaps rewards for him.

Make car rules.

Institute the rule that the car moves only when everyone in it is buckled in a seat belt. Say, "I'm sorry that your belt is not buckled. The car can't move until it is." Be prepared to wait until the passengers comply with your rule before you go.

Provide appropriate play materials.

Make sure you pack toys that are harmless to clothes and upholstery. Crayons are good, for instance, but felt tip pens are discouraged because they may mark the upholstery if accidentally dropped. If you're taking public transportation, provide activities that can be used in a controlled space, are as quiet as possible, and can hold attention for long periods.

Familiarize your child with your travel plans.

Discuss your travel plans with your child so he will know how long you will be gone, what will happen to his room while you're away, and when you will return. Show him maps and photos of your destination. Talk to him about the people, scenery, and events you will see and the things you will do. Share personal stories and souvenirs from past visits to the destination. Compare your destination to one your child is familiar with to ease his possible anxiety over going to someplace unknown to him.

Personally involve your child traveler.

Allow your child to be a part of the preparation and trip execution. Enlist his help in packing his clothing, selecting carry-on toys, carrying the tote bag, staying close in the terminal, etc.

Establish rules of conduct for your child to follow during the upcoming visit.

Before you leave, tell your child which rules, games, and activities will and won't be allowed while visiting Grandma or Aunt Helen. For example, make a "noise rule," an "exploring rule," a "pool rule," and a "restaurant rule" for intermediate stops and destinations.

Solving the Problem

Praise good behavior.

Praise good behavior frequently and provide rewards for staying in car seats. Say, for instance, "I really like the way you are looking at all the trees and houses. It's really a pretty day. We can soon get out and play in the park because you have sat in your car seat so nicely."

Stop the car if your child gets out of the seat or unbuckles the belt.

Make sure your child realizes that your car seat rule will be enforced, and that the consequences will be the same every time the rule is violated.

Play car games.

Count objects, recognize colors, and look for animals, for example, to involve your child in the process of getting from here to there. His attention span (and yours) will not last long on one game, so make a list of fun stuff before you leave; pull out several per hour, rotating games so your child's interest and yours will be assured.

Make frequent rest stops.

Your restless preschooler is usually at his best when mobile, so being restrained for hours in a car, plane, or train is not well suited to his adventurous nature. Give him time to physically let off steam in a roadside park, for example, or you'll find him verbally rebelling when you least desire or expect it.

Monitor snacks on long trips.

Highly sugared or carbonated foods can not only increase a child's activity level but may also increase potential nausea. Stick to protein snacks or lightly salted ones, instead of sugared ones, for the sake of health and happiness.

Use Grandma's Rule.

Let your child know that good behavior on trips will bring rewards. Say, "When you've sat in your seat and talked with us without whining, then we'll stop and get something to drink," for example, if your child has been whining for a drink.

Don't make promises you may not fulfill.

Don't be too specific about what your child may see on your travels, because he may hold you to it. If you say you may see a bear in Yellowstone, for example, and you don't, you will probably hear whining cries of "But you promised I'd see a bear" when you leave the park.

CAR WARS

Jerry and Leah Sterling wanted a vacation with the family that was just like the vacations they had each taken when they were young. But traveling with their children, three-year-old Tracy and five-year-old Travis was more like punishment than a joy ride.

The backseat of the car became a fist-fighting arena, and their children's screaming always led to threats and then to spanking. But the Sterlings often felt just as angry after the punishment as they did before, and they felt absolutely hopeless about finding a solution to their traveling problems.

So the Sterlings decided to develop new rules for traveling and to test the rules out on ordinary trips to the grocery store, to the park, or to friends' homes. They searched through the children's toys to find some safe toys that their kids could play with without supervision, and they explained the new policy for car trips.

"Kids," they began, "we are going to go to the grocery store. When you've sat in your seats and talked with us nicely all the way there, you each can pick out your favorite kind of juice."

The Sterlings praised their kids when they followed the rule: "Thanks for getting so quiet; I really like the way you're not whining and hurting each other!" But generally the plan failed miserably the first time, and the kids didn't get a treat at the store.

It only took two more "local" tests for both children to behave well in the car, receive praise for their efforts, and be rewarded for their good behavior.

Two weeks later, the Sterling family began its two-hour trek to Grandma's, the longest trip in the car since the practice sessions had begun. The children knew what was expected of them and what rewards awaited them along the way and at their destination—all of which made going over the river and through the woods a lot more fun.

RESISTING CAR SEATS

Car seats and seat belts are the number-one enemy of millions of freedom-loving preschoolers. These adventurous spirits don't understand why they must be strapped down, but they *can* understand the rule that the car doesn't go if the belt's not on or they are not in their car seat. Ensure your child's safety every time she gets in a car by enforcing the belts-on rule. The seat belt habit will become second nature to your child, as a passenger today and a driver tomorrow, if you are not wishywashy with this life-or-death rule.

Children who are not buckled in a seat belt will continue to travel forward if the car stops suddenly. They will hit anything in their path—the dashboard, the windshield, or the back of the front seat—with the impact equivalent to a one-story drop for each ten miles per hour the car is traveling. Even though the dashboard and back of the front seat are padded, the impact of a crash at fifty-five miles per hour can do considerable damage to small bodies.

Check car seats. Approved car safety seats and seat belts have weight and age specifications to make car travel as safe for your child as possible. Some seats for infants are too small for older children; some children can and will sit in seat belts or the newer booster seats, rather than an infant car seat.

The leading cause of death in children is trauma from automobile accidents. Much of that trauma could have been prevented by children wearing car restraints. So don't compromise your rule about being belted, or you may be compromising your child's life away.

PREVENTING THE PROBLEM

Give your child room to breathe and see.

Make sure the seat is as comfortable to sit in and see out of as yours. Check whether the eye level of your child allows her to see the passing countryside. Check how much room she has to move her hands and legs and still be safely strapped.

Make a rule—the car will not go unless everyone is belted in.

The sooner (from birth) you begin enforcing this rule, the more accustomed your child will be to the idea of sitting in a car seat or wearing a seat belt.

Make safety age-appropriate.

Make sure your child is aware of why she's graduating to a bigger seat or to just using a seat belt to make her proud of being strapped in. Say, "You are getting to be so grown-up. Here is your new safety seat for the car."

Don't complain about having to wear a seat belt.

Casually telling your spouse or friend that you hate wearing a seat belt, for example, gives your child the cue to resist her belt too.

Conduct a training program.

Take short drives around the neighborhood with one parent or friend driving and the other rewarding your child's sitting nicely in the car seat, to let your child know how you expect her to act in a car. Tell your child "You're staying in your safety belt so nicely today," or "Nice sitting," while patting and stroking her.

SOLVING THE PROBLEM

WHAT TO DO

Belt yourself in.

Make sure you wear the seat belt and point out how your child is wearing one just like yours, to make your seat-belted child feel she's not alone in her temporary confinement. If you don't wear a belt, your child will not understand why she has to.

Praise staying in the seat belt.

If you ignore your child while she's riding nicely, she will look for ways to get your attention, including trying to get out of her seat, which she knows brings you to her side. Keep your child out of car trouble by letting her know you are "with" her in her back seat, for example. Talk and play word games, as well as praise how nicely she's sitting.

Be consistent.
Stop the car as immediately and safely as possible every time your child gets out of her car seat or seat belt, to teach her that the rule will be enforced. Say, "The car can go again when you stay in your seat and are belted so you will be safe."

Divert your child's attention.
Try activities such as number or word games, peekaboo, or song singing, for example, so your child won't try to get out of her seat because she needs something to do.

WHAT NOT TO DO

Don't attend to your child's behavior other than unfastening the belt or getting out of the car seat.
Not giving attention to your crying or whining child while she's still belted in helps her see that there's no benefit in protesting the seat-belt rule. Say to yourself, "I know my child is safer in her car seat and will only fight it temporarily. Her safety is my responsibility and I am fulfilling it best by enforcing the seat-belt rule."

UNBUCKLED ALAN

Harry Brenner loved to take his four-year-old son Alan on errands with him—until his son figured out how to get his father's undivided attention by unbuckling his car seat belt and jumping around in the back seat.

"Don't you *ever* undo that belt again, young man!" Mr. Brenner ordered when he saw that his son had gotten free.

But simply demanding that Alan stay put didn't solve the problem, so Mr. Brenner decided that harsher, more physical punishment was necessary. Though he had never spanked his son before, he gave him a swift swat on his bottom whenever he found him roaming unbuckled around the back seat.

To accomplish the spanking, however, Mr. Brenner had to stop the car, and every time he did that, he noticed that Alan scrambled back to his seat to avoid being walloped. So Mr. Brenner decided to see if he could just stop the car and announce that they would not continue until Alan's belt was buckled. His son would be made to suffer the consequences of his misbehavior.

He tried this new method the next time they were on their way to the park. "We can go to the park when you are back in your seat and belted in," Mr. Brenner explained. "If you get out of your seat, I'll have to stop the car," he continued. "It's not safe for you to be unbuckled."

A few miles from home, his son unlocked himself as usual, and Mr. Brenner kept his part of the bargain by stopping the car. He didn't spank his son; he simply repeated the new rule and crossed his fingers, hoping that Alan would get back into his seat, since Mr. Brenner knew he was eager to go to the park.

He was right. Alan returned to his seat and calmly buckled himself in again. Mr. Brenner told him, "Thanks for getting back into your seat," and they drove on to the park without incident.

That didn't end the problem, however, and the next time Alan released himself, Mr. Brenner was so angry he was tempted to yell and scream again, but he stuck to his new method. By continuing to include him in his conversations and by praising his good car behavior, he once again began to enjoy outings with his son, assured that they were traveling in safety.

CHILDPROOFING CHECKLIST

Alarming statistics show that accidents are the largest single cause of death in children from birth to age fifteen. Most accidents to children stem from the child's normal, healthy curiosity.

Chances of getting hurt increase as the child grows. Hazards multiply as a baby learns to creep, crawl, walk, climb, and explore. Often accidents occur when parents are not aware of their child's capabilities and capacities at his specific stage of development.

The following checklist identifies steps that parents must take to prevent home accidents.

- [ ] Install childproof latches on all cabinets and drawers that contain dangerous objects.

- [ ] Crawl through the house on your hands and knees to spot enticing hazards to be remedied.

- [ ] Plug empty electrical outlets with plastic plugs designed for this purpose.

- [ ] Remove unused extension cords.

- [ ] Move a large sofa or chair in front of electrical outlets that have cords plugged in them.

- [ ] If small tables or other furnishings are not sturdy or have sharp corners, store them away until your child is older.

- [ ] Place dangerous household substances, such as detergents, cleaning fluids, razor blades, matches, and medicines, well out of reach in a locked cabinet.

- [ ] Install a proper screen on a fireplace.
- [ ] Always use a correct car seat in your automobile.
- [ ] Regularly check toys for sharp edges or small broken pieces.
- [ ] Check the floor for small objects that your child could swallow or choke on.
- [ ] Put a gate on the stairway to prevent unsupervised play on the stairs.
- [ ] Never leave your baby unattended on a changing table, in the bathtub, on a couch, on your bed, in an infant seat or high chair, on the floor, or in a car.
- [ ] Have syrup of ipecac on hand to induce vomiting in case your child swallows a noncorrosive poison.
- [ ] Place small, fragile tabletop items out of your child's reach.
- [ ] Keep the door to the bathroom closed at all times.
- [ ] Keep plastic bags and small objects (pins, buttons, nuts, hard candy, money) out of reach at all times.
- [ ] Make sure toys, furniture, and walls are finished in lead-free paint. Check labels to make sure toys are nontoxic.
- [ ] Teach the word *hot* as early as you can. Keep your child away from the hot oven, iron, vent, fireplace, wood stove, barbecue grill, cigarettes, cigarette lighter, and hot tea and coffee cups.
- [ ] Always turn pot handles inward when cooking.
- [ ] Always raise crib sides in the up position when your baby (even a tiny infant) is in the crib.
- [ ] Do not hang a tablecloth off a table when your small child is close by.
- [ ] Never tie toys to a crib or playpen; your baby could strangle on the string. Also, never put a string on a pacifier and around your baby's neck.

APPENDIX 2
FEEDING GUIDE FOR YOUNG CHILDREN

Child-size servings are suggested below to help you judge what amount to give your child. It is better to offer small servings and let your child ask for second helpings than to give her large servings.

	1 to 2 Years	2 to 3 Years	3 to 5 Years
Milk	Up to 1/2 cup	6-ounce cup or glass (3/4 cup)	6-ounce cup or glass (3/4 cup)
Juice	Up to 1/2 cup	3- to 4-ounce glass (1/3 to 1/2 cup)	4-ounce glass (1/2 cup)
Egg	1 medium	1 medium	1 medium
Meat	Up to 1/2 cup cut-up meat	About as much as a cooked meat patty 3 inches across, 1/2 inch thick (6 to 7 patties per pound)	About as much as a cooked meat patty 3 inches across, 1/2 inch thick (6 to 7 patties per pound)
Cereal	2 tablespoons cooked; 1/3 cup ready-to-eat	2 tablespoons cooked; 1/3 cup ready-to-eat	1/4 cup cooked; 1/2 cup ready-to-eat
Bread	1/2 slice	1/2 slice	1 slice
Vegetables and Fruits	1/2 medium apple, tomato, orange; 1 to 2 tablespoons others	1/2 medium apple, tomato, orange; 1 to 2 tablespoons others	1/2 to 1 medium apple, tomato, orange; 2 to 4 tablespoons others

Ready for School?
by Marge Eberts and Peggy Gisler

A recent survey of kindergarten teachers warns: Don't force-feed reading and math to your preschooler! This practical book offers a low-pressure way to prepare your child for kindergarten that really works. Learn how to help your child learn the basic skills that are a must for kindergarten *without* turning into a "teacher." Eberts and Gisler are former teachers who write "Dear Teacher," a nationally syndicated newspaper column. They show how much fun it can be to share learning activities with your preschooler.

Order #1360

Free Stuff for Kids
by the Free Stuff Editors

Here's the 1994 edition of the best-selling children's activitiy book in the U.S. Revised and updated, it features hundreds of terrific free and up-to-a-dollar items that kids can send away for by mail, including special environmental offers. It's a terrific incentive for kids to practice their writing skills! No wonder it has sold over 2.5 million copies!

Order #2190

Baby & Child Medical Care
edited by Terril Hart, M.D.

Every first aid or medical problem your child suffers seems like an emergency. That's why you need this fast, easy-to-read, useful source of medical information at your fingertips. Newly revised, this book provides illustrated step-by-step instructions that show you what to do and tell you when to call your doctor. Its visual approach makes Dr. Spock look like it's from the "horse and buggy" era, by comparison.

Order #1159

Practical Parenting Tips
by Vicki Lansky

Here's the #1 selling collection of helpful hints for parents of babies and small children. It contains 1001 parent-tested tips for dealing with diaper rash, nighttime crying, toilet training, temper tantrums, and traveling with tots that will help you save trouble, time, and money.

Order #1179

Feed Me! I'm Yours
by Vicki Lansky

This classic cookbook for parents of infants, toddlers, and tots contains over 200 time-tested recipes for making baby food from scratch and preparing nutritional snacks for preschoolers. Spiral bound to lay flat—a handy feature since many mothers say they "live out of it." No wonder it has sold over 2.5 million copies.

Order #1109

The Joy of Parenthood
by Jan Blaustone

This book contains hundreds of wise, warm, and inspirational "nuggets" of wisdom to help prepare parents for the pleasures and challenges ahead. Twenty-four touching black and white photos help convey the joy of parenthood, and make this a delightful book to give or receive.

Order #3500

Baby & Child Emergency First Aid Handbook
edited by Mitchell J. Einzig, M.D.

The director of Medical Education at the Minneapolis Children's Medical Center provides the clearest and simplest illustrated, step-by-step instructions available anywhere on how to help your child in an emergency—before the ambulance arrives or the hospital can be reached.

Order #1380

Order Form

Qty.	Title	Author	Order No.	Unit Cost	Total
	Baby & Child Emergency First Aid	Einzig, M.	1380	$15.00	
	Baby & Child Medical Care	Hart, T.	1159	$8.00	
	Baby Journal	Bennett, M.	3172	$10.00	
	Baby Name Personality Survey	Lansky/Sinrod	1270	$8.00	
	Best Baby Name Book	Lansky, B.	1029	$5.00	
	Best Baby Shower Book	Cooke, C.	1239	$7.00	
	Dads Say the Dumbest Things!	Lansky, B.	4220	$6.00	
	David, We're Pregnant!	Johnston, L.	1049	$6.00	
	Discipline W/out Shouting/Spanking	Wyckoff/Unell	1079	$6.00	
	Do They Ever Grow Up?	Johnston, L.	1089	$6.00	
	Feed Me! I'm Yours	Lansky, V.	1109	$8.00	
	First-Year Baby Care	Kelly, P.	1119	$7.00	
	Free Stuff For Kids	Free Stuff Editors	2190	$5.00	
	Getting Organized For Your New Baby	Bard, M.	1229	$5.00	
	Grandma Knows Best	McBride, M.	4009	$6.00	
	Hi Mom! Hi Dad!	Johnston, L.	1139	$6.00	
	Joy of Parenthood	Blaustone, J.	3500	$6.00	
	Kids Pick the Funniest Poems	Lansky, B.	2410	$14.00	
	Maternal Journal	Bennett, M.	3171	$10.00	
	Moms Say the Funniest Things!	Lansky, B.	4280	$6.00	
	More Free Stuff For Kids	Free Stuff Editors	2191	$5.00	
	Mother Murphy's Law	Lansky, B.	1149	$4.50	
	Pregnancy, Childbirth, & Newborn	Simkin/Whalley/Keppler	1169	$12.00	
	Ready for School?	Eberts/Gisler	1360	$5.95	
	Work. Woman's Guide/Breastfeeding	Dana/Price	1259	$7.00	
				Subtotal	
			Shipping and Handling		
			MN residents add 6.5% sales tax		
				Total	

YES! Please send me the books indicated above. Add $2.00 shipping and handling for the first book and 50¢ for each additional book. Add $2.50 to total for books shipped to Canada. Overseas postage will be billed. Allow up to 4 weeks for delivery. Send check or money order payable to Meadowbrook Press. No cash or C.O.D.'s please. Prices subject to change without notice. **Quantity discounts available upon request.**

Send book(s) to:

Name_____

Address _____

City _____ State _____ Zip_____

Telephone (___) _____

Purchase order number (if necessary) _____

Payment via:

☐ Check or money order payable to Meadowbrook Press (No cash or C.O.D.'s please.)

 Amount enclosed $ _____

☐ Visa (for orders over $10.00 only.)   ☐ MasterCard (for orders over $10.00 only.)

Account # _____

Signature _____ Exp. Date _____

A FREE Meadowbrook catalog is available upon request.

You can also phone us for orders of $10.00 or more at 1-800-338-2232.

Mail to: Meadowbrook, Inc.
18318 Minnetonka Boulevard, Deephaven, Minnesota 55391
(612) 473-5400   Toll-Free 1-800-338-2232   Fax (612) 475-0736